Revival 2000!

Mona Johnian

Revival 2000! By Mona Johnian
ISBN 0-929685-52-0
Copyright © 1995 by Mona Johnian

Published by:
Superior Books
73 Pine Street
Woburn, MA 01801

Edited by:
Liberty Savard

Book and cover design:
Terri Caprini

Contents

Introduction v

1. A Radical Acceleration of Change 1
2. A Table in the Presence of My Enemies............9
3. Does Man Want Real Revival? 21
4. Laughter and More Laughter 35
5. Can Men Stop Revival? 49
6. A Divine Encounter 67
7. The Sanctifying Work of Revival 77
8. Set Among Princes 89
9. When God Speaks 103
10. Stop Whining and Start Burning 119
11. Life-Changing Worship 135
12. Hallelujah! 147

Prologue...159

Introduction

Revival is not coming. It has already arrived in people and places around the world! The Christian Teaching and Worship Center in Boston, Massachusetts, has been in constant revival since November of 1993. It is a spiritual awakening that came suddenly and has remained with incredible evidence. We are convinced that we are in the early stages of a revival that will eventually cover the entire earth.

The heart of this book is to challenge the Church that this outpouring is true revival and to plead with God's people to enter into the glorious refreshing. This book is a description of the divine invasion we are experiencing at Christian Teaching and Worship Center, yet it is not confined to the four walls of our church building. We see a stirring that is leaping out like tiny sparks from a fire that will eventually ignite into a roaring flame. What is happening is scriptural and it is spreading.

Pentecost started in one small city, but it spread over the earth through the zeal and commitment of those who were set on fire by its power and its program. Revivals are agendas from God, brought by His Holy Spirit. They are initiated by God, but they affect His people personally, as well as corporately, and they are carried out through His people in the changing experience of individual lives. Unlike man's stereotypical definition of a revival being a series of church services, true revivals always change lives.

Much of the division over the revival now visiting God's people is initially being centered around the great joy and holy laughter flowing out of the captives as they are being set free. As the revival develops, division will arise over other issues as well. If you were God and wanted to let your people know that you were bringing revival to them, how would you go about it? When the Church prays for revival—which it has been doing earnestly for many years—how is the Holy Spirit to let them know He is present and answering their prayers except He express Himself tangibly, obviously and personally?

In January of 1995, my eighty-six-year-old Southern Baptist aunt was sitting in her country store where she has been sitting for the past forty years. Once a strong, commanding lady, disease has shrunk her stature by some seven inches to a height of four feet and eleven inches tall. During one perfectly normal day as my aunt was going about her usual routine of reading in between customers, an invisible but very real presence appeared and saturated her entire body.

"All of a sudden, every pain left my body and I was engulfed with a sense of total health," she later said. "I felt like a young girl again. As I got up and began to walk around, joy flooded me repeatedly. I could have buried every one of my children without a tear. It was a total peace, happiness and joy unlike anything I've ever experienced. It was a tangible presence that remained with me for about an hour."

God is drawing near to His people. His agenda has never been to refresh human structures and human institutions, but His will is to refresh His people, one by one, whether they are en masse or all alone. He is visiting the earth in special ways with increasing frequency, making house calls at some unique addresses, personally and corporately. The time has come for a new definition of revival.

A genuine, worldwide revival is not confined to the setting of the Church. One unique feature of this outpouring is the unorthodox places and people who are being affected by it. People who have had no witness are seeking God. Churches that have not especially prayed for revival are being invaded—ours is one of them! It is a sovereign move outside of man's guidelines for church growth and steps to victorious living. The best strategies of man cannot run with what we see happening. God has loosed himself from man's agendas. He is moving as He wishes.

The Holy Spirit has come with revival to manifest the presence of God and to make Him visibly seen and known and experienced. Those who receive revival will enter into an anointing that shows. Those who resist revival will show their rebellion. Revival does indeed expose the true spirit of a man, a church or a nation. Those who genuinely wish to promote the glory of God will lay down their lives and commit to the will of the Spirit. Those who wish to retain their own glory, or the glory of the past, will take various measures to stop the flow or eliminate themselves from its influence. The question the Church needs to address at this moment in history is this: *"Are we going to flow with this revival or will we seek to stop it?"*

1

A Radical Acceleration of Change

Sixty thousand people gathered in Boston at the World Trade Center computer show where the keynote speaker was renowned physicist Stephen Hawking from Great Britain. Hawking, who is confined to a wheelchair with a degenerative disease, is Professor of Mathematics at Cambridge University, the same post once held by Sir Isaac Newton.

Mr. Hawking noted that because of the phenomenal ability of computers to store and transmit information, knowledge is accumulating far faster than man can handle it:

> "This is beginning to cause problems. We still have the instincts and aggressive impulses we had in the caveman days. Intelligence does not guarantee survival of a species. Maybe it says something about human behavior that the only form of life we have created so far is destructive. Talk about creating life in our own image!"

Human intellect is glutted. We have now arrived at a time when we know more than we can handle. We have long worshipped at the shrine of human intelligence, and our knowledge has turned destructive. What the world desperately needs is a revival of the spirit. Herein lies the danger: The Church is now seriously divided over the beginnings of that revival. What will we do? How are we going to respond? This is the great question that now confronts the believing world.

The Church is a Vessel

If ministers and congregations understood this revival, they would not hesitate to give themselves to it. Just as Mary was the vessel who carried the child conceived by the Holy Spirit within herself, it is up to the Church to carry the conception of revival until it is fully birthed. Once birthed, the revival must then be nurtured from infancy into maturity if a great harvest is realized. Praying for revival prepares our hearts, but energy and time must be invested in revival itself if the Church will enter into spiritual refreshings for extended periods of time. Revivals are sent by God, but they are nurtured by those hungry for more of God.

Nothing that occurs on earth is as important as an outpouring of the Holy Spirit. Nothing of eternal import happens without such an outpouring. The Holy Spirit has come to this earth to bring the weight of God to bear upon the present direction man is taking, individually and collectively. The spirit world is shaking at the sound of revival. Every institution will shake before it is over...beginning with the Church itself!

Can Man Hinder?

Can men's actions in fact hinder the Spirit of God from operating in their lives? In the first covenant between God and man, Samuel records what appears to be a resounding yes! Saul was anointed to be the king on whose throne the

Messiah would one day rule the whole earth. Because of greed and witchcraft, Saul rejected his anointing. And Samuel said to Saul, *"Thou hast done foolishly: thou hast not kept the commandment of the Lord thy God, which he commanded thee: for now would the Lord have established thy kingdom upon Israel for ever. But now thy kingdom shall not continue: the Lord hath sought him a man after his own heart, and the Lord hath commanded him to be captain over his people, because thou hast not kept that which the Lord commanded thee"* (1 Sam. 13:13,14 KJV).

From the new covenant, we also have the glaring example of the Holy Spirit turning away (for a time) from the nation of Israel to the Gentiles. Officially speaking, Israel missed the revival of Pentecost, and many have been their woes as they continue to wait for God to *"...pour upon the house of David, and upon the inhabitants of Jerusalem, the spirit..."* once again (Zech. 12:10 KJV).

The Holy Spirit cannot be stopped from carrying out God's ultimate program, but revivals can be hindered, even stopped from happening in certain places. Although Jesus had the power to do anything, He did not do many spiritual works in Nazareth because of unbelief. He demonstrated this power in other cities—but not Nazareth, for the Nazarenes hindered the Spirit and missed the revival Jesus brought to their city.

Charles Finney was a man who both experienced and examined hindrances to revival. The spearhead of one of America's greatest periods of revival, Finney wrote with a pen dripping with fiery proof of the greatness of the Spirit of God. That we may avoid the bitter fruit of pride and apathy at this moment of spiritual awakening, this book draws on some of the wisdom of this eloquent former attorney turned evangelist from 19th century America. Finny wrote:

> "Some have talked very foolishly on this subject, as if nothing could hinder a genuine revival.... A revival is the work of God, and so is a crop of wheat; and God is as much dependent on the use of 'means' in one case as the other. And therefore a revival is as likely to be injured as a wheat field" (*Revivals of Religion*, Charles G. Finney, CBN University Press, pg. 292).

In other words, God uses men to accomplish His works on earth both naturally as well as supernaturally. God gives seed; men cultivate the ground and plant the seed. God sends the sun and rains, men harvest a wheat crop. When men prepare and maintain the spiritual soil for the Spirit of God to move in outpouring, God moves. When men cease to maintain the soil, spiritual or natural, there will be crop failure. Hardness will set in, the seed will not germinate and harvest will not come.

Hindrances to Revival

Finney made a list of things that will stop a revival. According to his observation and experience:

1) "A revival will stop whenever the Church believes it is going to cease.... Nothing is more fatal to a revival than for its friends to predict that it is going to stop" (ibid., 292-293).

When the Spirit first began to visit our church with an awakening, He found friends immediately. Many in the congregation began to enter in as best they understood. Some chose to observe, some complained, some left. As time has gone by, one by one the observers and complainers have also begun entering in as we have discovered that God can be experienced, heard from, enjoyed and touched. It has been such a joyful satisfaction that I refused to think about its ending.

Now that I have read Charles Finney's experiences with hindrances to revival, I understand why grace has kept us from projecting the end of the outpouring. The pitcher is in God's hands. It is not for you and me to speculate how long He will pour His revival waters of blessing forth.

Jesus walked in revival all the way past the cross and into hell where He took the keys of death and hell from Satan and his kingdom. The Apostle Paul experienced supernatural moves and the power of the Holy Spirit to the day of his earthly departure. He had angelic visitations, miraculous deliverances, healings, raising of the dead and was raised from the dead himself. Paul never experienced ministry burnout, for he lived in constant revival. Everywhere he went revival broke out and turned Satan's world upside down. The Apostle Paul never went around only talking about what God used to do. He said, *"For our gospel came not unto you in word only, but also in power, and in the Holy Ghost, and in much assurance..."* (1 Thess. 1:5 KJV).

"But revival fires die out!" some will call out to whoever would listen. But I ask them, "Did the revival die out of Jesus? Or the apostles? Did the revival die out of Wesley? Or Dwight L. Moody?" I'm not convinced that revivals die, so much as men put out the flame by their own attitude and behavior toward the Reviver when times of *"refreshing shall come from the presence of the Lord"* (Acts 3:19 KJV). Incredible as it may seem, the contemporary Church quickly tires of the manifested presence of God when His presence requires extended worship services. Only those who are consumed with what God is doing seem not to notice. To those who would abandon their souls to their God, three hours seems brief when He is manifesting His glory. Time is nothing, relatively speaking, to those who are hungry for His presence. Revival takes time if good things are to come from it.

I went down the hallway of the church with a joyful shout one morning. "Revival is wonderful!" I said as I passed a staff person.

He smiled, "Yes it is. I like to feel good."

"It's more than feeling good," I replied. "It's life changing." As I walked on, the Holy Spirit began to speak to me about how many Christians are afraid that feeling good is only emotionalism. But revival is a time when the presence of God is manifesting among His people, and it is normal to 'feel good' in the presence of a good God. Good feelings during worship come from the real presence of a good God.

Evidence of Real Things

The good things that happen in an outpouring of the Holy Spirit defy human explanation. God sent me to a major conference in New Jersey to witness to the fact of the "great awakening" the Church is entering. More than 128 nations were represented at this conference. As ministers came by my booth, both my assistant and I shared the impact of nine months of a fresh anointing on our Boston congregation. One pastor from Yugoslavia stopped and inquired about the revival. We showed this pastor my book *"The Fresh Anointing"* and encouraged him to come back for a copy. After he left we determined to give him the book upon his return, but we never saw him again.

In the meantime, while I was still in New Jersey, one of our members in Boston was going out of town and would be attending church somewhere else. As she passed by our bookstore, the Holy Spirit said, *"Go inside and buy two 'Fresh Anointing' books to take with you, and you will reach a great host of people with them.*" Surprised by the word, Shirley nevertheless obeyed and took the books to Maine. As she sat down in the church service where she was visiting, a pastor from Yugoslavia was introduced as the visiting speaker. Shirley heard an inner voice speak to her, *"Give the 'Fresh Anointing' books to him."*

Afterwards when Shirley went up to present the books, the Yugoslavian pastor's eyes filled with tears as he said, "I saw this book in New Jersey, but I could not afford to buy a copy." From New Jersey, by way of Massachusetts to Maine, God saw to it that knowledge of revival would be taken to Yugoslavia. This is one of dozens of reports we receive each week about the direct leading of God, or intervention of God in specific ways, since revival began. We are seeing God reach across international boundaries, national boundaries and denominational boundaries with this revival.

> "I was searching for this revival from Florida to Maryland when I heard it was at the Christian Teaching and Worship Center. In April, I came for a look. Right away Paul pointed that bow of his at me (after playing his violin, Pastor Paul sometimes uses his bow to point). My feet wanted to run, my whole body was shaking and down I went hearing the words, 'Lord, heal her body.' I tried to get up, but Paul pointed that bow again and back down I went. Then I started to laugh and I'm still getting fixed. My granddaughter got saved and my daughter was set free from drinking a pint of vodka daily."

A call came from a happy young man in a large New England Baptist Church, who has loved every revival service he has attended. He excitedly gave the following testimony:

> "Yesterday, during worship in my church, I received an anointing to bring a prophecy to our congregation. So I asked for and received permission from my pastor to bring the word.

> 'We cannot put God in a box,' my pastor said. When I brought the word, holy laughter broke out in the congregation. I started praying, the anointing came and people all over the church began to fall under the power of the Spirit."

Without question, we are in a period of accelerated change. To those bent on maintaining the "status quo," what is happening around the world in the Church probably seems radical and many spiritual leaders and lay people want to hold back or "wait and see." Some have already begun to predict its end. But since man did not initiate the outpouring of God's Holy Spirit, we must not attempt to stop it or predict its ending. Too many good things are finally happening in the lives of people hungry for a touch from God.

2

A Table in the Presence of My Enemies

"We ought to obey God rather than oppose Him"
(Abraham Lincoln).

In the Apostle John's Book of Revelation, Jesus compared the Church to a golden lampstand. During one of our worship services I saw a vision of a golden lampstand lying on its side with the oil dripping out and the flame impaired. The Spirit then said, *"I am setting my Church upright. As I pass through the congregations I am illuminating the dark places of each life. Once my people have been spiritually positioned and the flame rekindled, then my Church will pass through the world and bring light into it."*

When the divine council of the Godhead determines that *"times of refreshing"* are coming, the Holy Spirit is sent down to accomplish specific goals and objectives in the Church and in the world. God alone determines how the Holy Spirit will conduct the process when He arrives. The Church has long entreated God for revival, but history shows that signs of the moving of the Spirit are viewed with skepticism, if not outright rejection.

"Emotionalism! Disorder!" are two historical cries of people whose form and formality are suffering an invasion. When this cry overtakes the spirit of the people, the Church once again attempts to stuff God back into their mental concepts of what is proper and what is right. But we can be thankful that God will not allow His Holy Spirit to endure such an entrapment.

Genuine revival *will* disrupt the ordinary flow of the worship service and the life of the worshiper. When the great revivalist George Whitefield came from England to America in 1740, one of the criticisms used against him was his open air meetings. Men were totally unaccustomed to worshipping anywhere except inside a church building. Added to this breach of church etiquette was Mr. Whitefield's practice of:

> "...singing hymns in the public roads, when riding from town to town" (*Revivals of Religion*, Charles G. Finney, CBN University Press, pg. 273).

Religious form said the common road was not a proper place to be singing hymns of worship. One distinguished Boston minister (referring to Mr. Whitefield's unorthodox methods) said to him, "I am sorry to see you in Boston."

Whitefield responded, "So is the devil," and he continued his revival practices.

Revivals in the Church distress the devil. Men who get released from "form to faith" are ready to move mountains and Satan does what he can to stir up opposition to any hint of mountain moving power. A young man came to me saying, "Why don't you do more correcting of the excesses that have come since revival?"

I responded, "Because over-legislation of this move of God in its infancy will kill it." Finney previously responded to those who voiced similar concerns and said they were "being taken up with the evils instead of the excellencies of the blessed work."

Charles Finney and Revival

When it comes to revival in modern history, perhaps no man stands out like the agnostic lawyer from New York named Charles Finney. After his conversion to Christ at age 35, Finney went on to lead one of the greatest eras of spiritual and moral awakening the United States of America has ever known. Following the "Great Awakenings" of Edwards and Whitefield one hundred years before him, Finney sparked a fire that literally set this nation ablaze with a spiritual awakening that saw more than 200,000 people born again. In one summer alone, as many as 10,000 people a week were being saved. In a revival flame that lasted ten years, thousands of people in all denominations came to salvation with dramatic moral, social and even political change resulting.

Out of his vast experience, Finney analyzed revival and wrote about it for the benefit of those who would experience other moves of God in the future. I believe we are some of those followers who need to take note of what Finney learned. Revivals are sent by God, but they must be received and acted upon by men if we are to benefit from what God offers. God is now pouring out His grace on a form-bound and slumbering Church that is set in a violent and radical generation. Help us, Lord, to respond mightily to this outpouring!

Pushing Beyond the Established Form

An echo from Rome, 2,000 years old, comes back to haunt every revival:

> *"And (they) brought them (Paul and Silas) to the magistrates, saying, "These men, being Jews, do exceedingly trouble our city, and teach customs, which are not lawful for us to receive, neither to observe, being Romans"* (Acts 16:20,21).

In other words, "This revival is not suitable for our tradition." How many times have we heard this remark since revival invaded our church in November of 1993? It is a remark that drove me to seek what the appropriate form of Christian worship really is. Does the Bible tell us how to conduct a worship service? According to Charles Finney:

> "We are left in the dark as to the measures pursued by the apostles and primitive preachers.... Go and preach the Gospel, and disciple all nations. No person can pretend to get any set of forms or particular directions as to measures out of this commission. Do it—the best way you can; ask wisdom from God; use the faculties He has given you; seek the direction of the Holy Ghost; go forward and do it.... It is preaching the Gospel which...stands out prominently as the great thing. The form is left out of the question" (ibid., 261-262).

From this observation, Finney then goes on to explain how the Protestants, and to some extent the Catholics, have arrived at their present form of worship. It helps to be reminded of what the religious men and women one- and two-hundred-years ago considered appropriate behavior for clergy and laymen. Most of us would be shocked to know that ministers in the United States used to be required to wear a "cocked hat, bands around their neck instead of a cravat, a wig and a gown." Without these clothes, the ministers were not considered fit to officiate. When ministers began to wear hats as other men, it grieved the older members of the congregations. They felt the minister was lowering his standard. According to Finney, the

Church has always had a "superstitious reverence for such things."

Invading the Forms

If we will be honest, worship for many Christians is not so much an experience with God as it is an experience with a form of religion. We are comfortable with our religious forms. True revival invades our forms. True revival brings the refreshing presence of God down into the religious atmosphere men have created and shakes us awake to spiritual realities. Then we either press into God or deliberately seek to kill the revival.

God will not compete for worship—it must be offered freely to Him or it is meaningless. So long as men are satisfied with anything less than His presence, God will give them over to their own comfortable ritual. But for those who are hungry for more of God, hungry enough to let go of anything and everything that hides the fullness of God's presence from them—they will be revived!

But the man-controlled faction of the Church has always resisted and fought surrendering to God's ways. For example, violent reactions occurred in the 1800s when the Church began to introduce hymns in addition to the singing of the Psalms. During those times, because there were only a few songs books, it was customary to "line sing." A deacon would read a Psalm or hymn line by line, and the congregation would repeat it or sing it after him. When hymnals were finally made available to everyone, the people cried that it was all confusion and disorder! How could they possibly worship unless a "liner" set the "holy" tone before them? Choirs were thought to be "great evils." Pitchpipes caused some to get up and leave the services. An organ in the house of God brought about grave ecclesiastical discussions. When the bass viol was brought into the house of God the people said:

> "Why, it is a fiddle...who can worship where there is a fiddle?" (ibid., 269).

The established form had become the "holy thing" in singing. Music from today's most conservative church would have been considered abominable 200 years ago, because every musical instrument had been given over to the world and considered evil. The Church took God's instruments and gave them to the world in spite of the Word which says:

> "Praise ye the Lord. Praise God in his sanctuary...Praise him with the sound of the trumpet...the psaltery and harp...the timbrel and dance...stringed instruments and organs...the loud cymbals...the high sounding cymbals. Let everything that hath breath praise the Lord..." (Psalm 150 KJV).

In the matter of church prayer, our spiritual forefathers only considered readings from the prayer book as decent and proper. Preaching without notes was considered profane. Laymen praying and exhorting during public assembly "agitated all New England and many other parts of the country." Anyone other than a member of the clergy speaking out during public assembly was thought to induce confusion. Of course women's prayer meetings were extensively opposed. The men were quite huffy about this, saying, "Why, I suppose the next thing will be to set them to preach!" (ibid., 270).

Until men deal with their reverence for the religious forms they have created, the Church will continue to have difficulty entering into great spiritual awakenings. In the words of Charles Finney:

"If we examine the history of the Church, we shall find that there never has been an extensive reformation except by new measures. Whenever the churches get settled down into a form of doing things, they soon get to rely upon the outward doing of it...while they lose the substance" (ibid., 283).

Keeping the Life Flowing

Anything living is always in a state of change. When daily growth and development cease, death sets in. Finney taught that it was not only the right but the duty of ministers to "adopt new measures for promoting revivals," in order to keep the life flowing.

We encounter both ministers and laymen who say, "If God wants me in this flow, it will happen." My question is this: If God wants people saved, will it happen by the same principle? If God is pouring out His Spirit, He is already doing His part. And so He is in these exciting days, but this does not mean that He will do your part and mine. Our effort without the Spirit is fruitless. Our effort invested into the flow of the Spirit produces results.

A call came to our church one Monday informing us that a key pastor of the area was coming to our service that evening. "No!" we said in disbelief. For various reasons our relationship with that pastor had gone sour years earlier and never recovered. The pastor came and that night there was such an outpouring of the Holy Spirit, our worship leader was literally intoxicated for more than two hours. People were lying all over the auditorium laughing. Some were receiving prayer for healing. After the sermon had been delivered; the service was drawing to a close when the visiting pastor came forward and asked to say a word. Taking the microphone, he made a hallmark confession of humility and honesty:

"Few pastors really want to see or hear of great success in some other church, when they cannot seem to have that same success with their congregations. When I heard that there was revival at the Christian Teaching and Worship Center, I was annoyed. In all honesty, I have never really liked Paul and Mona. They never seemed to respond to my invitations to be a part of the fellowship of pastors here as I felt they should.

"I awoke this morning and prayed, 'Lord what do you want me to do today?' He said, *'Go to the Christian Teaching and Worship Center revival service tonight.'* So I am here tonight to get more of this anointing! Would you lay hands on me?"

What rejoicing went up from the congregation that night! What celebrating! When Paul laid hands on the pastor, he immediately fell to the floor and the Spirit began to pour forth a beautiful "Song of the Lord" about unity in the body of Christ. Only God can bring about true unity in His Church. Unity comes from the heart of God. No program can successfully address this vital issue of unity, but the Spirit can and is.

For years Paul and I tried to establish key connections with people and situations we knew would cause the Word to go out more abundantly, but until the revival came—we were unable to "make" it happen. Now it is as if "connection crews" are working twenty-four hours a day! Literally, what didn't work before, works now. Conversely, what worked before doesn't work as well now. Old methods are like outdated computers. They do a form of the job required, but they are incompatible with all the new equipment. They are certainly far less effective.

Even our teaching and preaching have been altered. There is more life and less classroom atmosphere coming from the pulpit. We teach, but the spirit of delivery somehow seems to make our speaking a present event. We are experiencing the Word of God as well as hearing it. We are experiencing the God of the Word as well as learning about Him. It is difficult to explain, but the sermon is more like a meal where, although only the head of the table is speaking, all are eating and enjoying the food together with the Host. The struggle with the Word is gone, the joy and life of the Word is changing us.

A Table Prepared

Revival intrudes upon all of man's time-honored systems. Pastor Paul and I flew several hours at the invitation of one minister to bring news of this fresh anointing. Once the Spirit began to flow in the host pastor's services, he became adamantly opposed to the proceedings. He handled his opposition by smiling before his congregation, while he blew up behind the scenes. On the last night of the conference the mood was heavy and ominous. We had no idea where we stood. The pastor finally sent word, "Do whatever you feel the Lord leads you to do," but all the while we knew he was dead set against what was certain to happen.

We began to pray, "Lord, these people belong to you. Don't let them be robbed." We would never have violated the pastor's orders. His feelings were opposed, his orders were "flow." Which should we follow?

The Spirit began to show me a large table suspended above the people. Then He spoke these words to me, "*I prepare a table for my people in difficult places. I prepare tables even 'in the presence of my enemies.' You must push beyond the present attitudes and circumstances, and put your heart on bringing down the table of the Lord's food for the people.*"

Without any idea of what to say, I stepped to the microphone and began to talk about the worthiness of God to be praised. Within five minutes the presence of the Spirit began to fall—the people listened for about ten minutes more and then without any encouragement for personal response, they leaped to their feet and started to shout, laugh, dance and rejoice greatly before the Lord. It was one of the greatest times of praise we have experienced since the revival began. Worship broke out into ministry and many were healed of infirmities that evening.

Later, as I reflected on the events of that service, God impressed a truth upon my spirit which has made a difference in my life. This present world system is under the control of God's archrival, Satan. The Church must learn to do God's work and serve from God's table in enemy territory. Circumstances will never be perfectly suited for kingdom work. But God has promised to feed us from His table in the very presence of the enemy. **This means that we will never be anywhere that God is not actively working with us.**

So, there is no one we can blame if we choose to back up or withdraw from our commission. We're there and God is there and that makes a majority in the middle of any enemy territory. What we need to do is push beyond our petty feelings and get in step with the Spirit so we can move on with the King's business.

It is easy to get discouraged and quit in this age that encourages everyone to blame someone else. "Well, we would have done great things, but 'they' interfered and ruined everything," has become our way out. God, however, allows no easy exits. He expects His people to stand steady and always be expecting Him to provide in the face of impossibilities. This is the choice of faith.

Helen's Answer

Revival is not only about pastors and unity, however. It is also about people's individual lives. At the beginning of the revival, when we were just beginning to enter into the joy, a woman in our congregation came up to me. This woman, works long, hard hours in one of the more popular restaurants here in Boston. "Someone stole my purse this week," she said. I knew Helen was the sole support of her house and that life had already treated her to some heartbreaking experiences. I murmured to myself, "Oh, Lord, not another blow," and reached for her hands.

Amazingly, even before we prayed, she said, "I believe God will restore my purse to me, and everything in it." In all honesty I did not have so much optimism. Hundreds of people daily pass through the restaurant where Helen works. I was certain God would help her out, but surely in some other way.

Nine months later, Helen stopped me in the hallway after service. She held up a purse as she said, "Remember when my bag was stolen? This week the police department called and said they had a handbag with my name in it. Not only was my name in my bag, but every credit card, my $32.00, my two Bibles...every single thing was there. Not one thing was missing!"

The truth is, Helen had been serving tables literally in the presence of her enemy when someone took her handbag. But the weight of God's Spirit pressed in on the thief until the goods were returned untouched. One has to wonder, though, what went through the thief's mind as he or she pondered the handbag's contents. For inside the bag Helen had written a note which read: "If you take this bag and do not return every article in it, you will be cursed!"

This is the God we worship. Not only is He the Lord of the golden vessels and purple tapestry of the Holy of Holies, but He is the God Who sees a struggling waitress about to be robbed and steps in and says, "*Not again! She sits at my table*." Fear of this God caused someone to respond wisely.

Calls come into our church every week from people who are learning how to eat and be happy in the presence of threatening circumstances. Until Jesus returns, the Church must continue to live in a world system that has great animosity towards God. Circumstances are rarely favorable for kingdom work. The world has little awards or rewards for dedicated workers of God. In the days ahead, it will award even fewer. We must make up our minds and set our wills to ignore the evils of this present world and be taken up with the "excellencies of the blessed work."

There is a work that brings blessing. And, as Helen warned her thief, a work that brings a curse. Revival is all about the excellent work that brings blessing.

3

Does Man Want Real Revival?

Moses once begged to see God's face. God denied his entreaty, but He did allow Moses to view more than he had ever seen before. Likewise, revivals reveal more of God than we have been allowed to see before. To reject or abuse times of such spiritual outpourings and revelation is to reject the intimate ovations of the world's greatest Lover. How brutish and adulterous are our hearts! To be so caught up in our religious programs, our ceremony and ritual, our personal ministries, that we would reject the outpourings of God himself is reprehensible.

Just to write on the subject of stopping revival strikes caution in my heart. To think of offending the Spirit of God, after He has so personally manifested Himself among us, is like discussing a plot to betray a spouse. It is a dirty deed against love. Yet, many people would rather fantasize about love itself than assume the responsibilities of being a lover. Some believers would rather be religious than to be in a relationship with the living, manifested God. They feel much more in control when they are only feeding their romantic notions about the God of history, instead of becoming intimate with the great Romancer of their souls.

Revival is a painful intrusion upon those who want such an "undisturbed religious fantasy." The eternally present, almighty God will not be assigned a number and a place in line while waiting for man to be ready for Him. He will break in upon the human scene whenever He chooses. This is scary to those who are withholding a complete commitment to God, for the great I AM, the God who refuses to stay quietly back in the dusty annals of history, is more than many "spiritual" men and women care to face today.

Charles Finney's experiences with revival led him to the belief that a revival will stop whenever the Church believes it is going to cease or consents that it should cease. After two or three weeks into revival at CTWC, our services began to waver. I saw our old program looming up to contest the new move of God's Spirit. Instead of entering into the fresh outpouring of joy, many of our people were wailing, "When is God going to do something for me?" Or, they were whispering behind the scenes, "When are we going to return to normal?"

I sensed panic on the horizon. I had tasted something wonderful and now I saw it fading, even before the majority had a chance to really enter in. In desperation I poured out myself before the Lord, entreating Him not to let the revival depart. Paul and I repented of everything the Holy Spirit brought to our awareness. We did everything we knew to do during our services to hear from God and to reverence His presence. We cried out for the thirsty who had come to drink from God and we begged Him to touch them.

In private, I even questioned God as to whether I was trying too hard. But I could not stop pressing relentlessly forward the best I knew how. Not a service went by that Paul and I did not preach revival and reaffirm our full commitment to it. At that point in time, we knew nothing of Charles Finney's points of hindrances to revival. We knew only our own desperation to see God's power flood our church until the whole of New England had been saturated. Only later did we get our confirmation that our struggle was right and typical of revival experiences. As Finney said:

> "When Christians love the work of God and the salvation of souls so well that they are distressed at the mere apprehension of a decline [of revival], it will drive them to agony and effort to prevent its ceasing; but if they see the danger and do not try to avert it, or to renew the work, they consent that it should stop" (*Revivals of Religion*, Charles G. Finney, CBN University Press, pg. 293).

When we see just one dark spot on fresh fruit, we know its days are numbered and we must partake of it quickly or lose it. Lagging interest, negative comments, growing indifference, are all spots in revival that must be addressed promptly by those in leadership. A good report must continually cancel out the negativisms or the "spots" will become obvious to the masses and a funeral dirge will begin. Paul and I labored to attend to the fruit of revival.

By the third month of revival, we were airborne and word was spreading. More people were entering into the revival, more people were coming to the church. By the ninth month, our worship was so alive with the anointing that people were literally crying out to God unashamedly. I saw strong, stoic men on their knees with tears streaming down their face. People were being set free of old bondages, salvations were taking place, physical healings began to increase and the physical walls of the sanctuary were pushed down to accommodate the crowd.

A Fresh Surge

When we were up to three services a week and looking for a place to move, I was shocked into an awareness one morning that several of our core membership were spiritually "dozing off" in the services. Others were becoming annoyed by the repeated manifestations of the Spirit, although they blamed it on the people. Some had settled into a comfortable spectator's chair and some had simply conditioned themselves to the fact of revival and were becoming desensitized to it.

Again I became desperate. During prayer God showed me that after the first wavering, we had received a surge of revival that got us airborne. Then we climbed to a comfortable altitude where we had again leveled off, and now it was time for another surge of power. We began to pray for another outpouring. This is when we received our first miracle of seeing near-blind eyes open. Pastors from other congregations began to come in seeking a closer walk with God and the liberty in our worship broke into a new dimension. We had fought off the tendency toward allowing revival to become mechanical and "common place" to us and God blessed our church.

The Church must dispel the notion that revivals are man-birthed, prayer-impelled, short-term moves of God that will naturally die out like the fads of the world. Revival must be promoted with genuine optimism every day if we want the Moses view of God and His will. Charles Finney warned the Church that "a revival will cease whenever Christians become mechanical in their attempts to promote it" (ibid., 294).

What causes a "living thing" to become mechanical and lifeless? All living things need attention and feeding, or they die. Marriages, relationships, churches—human bodies, minds, spirits—everything that is alive must all have food and attention or the life drains out of them. The Church is a living organism birthed by the Holy Spirit of God and He does not ever abandon it to feed or refresh itself. To grow and develop in strength and power, the Church requires food and refreshing that is native to it. Only the Spirit can nourish spirit. Revivals are special "feedings" from the Spirit of God, but the Church has to pick up its spiritual spoon and eat.

Pastors and ministers have the first responsibility in revival feedings. They must first taste and see for themselves that it is good, and then they must have the courage to take their people into change and new experiences. It takes boldness and steady faith to go into uncharted territory.

In the beginning days of this present move of God, Paul and I stood back and considered if this was "good" or not. We questioned seasoned ministers who have sown churches and works for more than twenty-five years. We inspected the fruit that was being produced by the joy and laughter breaking out in other congregations. Once we were satisfied by the fruit according to the Word of God, we began to eat of it ourselves. It tasted good, it satisfied and so we began serving it to our congregation. Real spiritual fruit began to come forth from these feedings, as the people began to go out and feed others. Word spread that one could go to the Christian Teaching and Worship Center and be touched by God, and people began coming from near and far. Life was being imparted.

Holy Spirit Alone Directs True Revival

We have exercised extreme caution not to utilize any schemes or man-conceived strategies to "help" the revival.

Various members of our staff have come to us saying, "Now that we're in revival, let us start a different prayer vigil. God is speaking to me to pray more."

"Then pray more," we answered, "but we do not feel the need to establish a new program." Having begun in the Spirit, we are determined not to try now to perfect the revival by the flesh. We should all pray more in these glory-filled days—but we will not build shrines of programs that others may copy to enhance God's revival. Frank Bartleman, of the 1907 Azusa Street visitation, wrote:

> "Past services now became a very blank to me...I began again for God, as though I had never accomplished anything. I felt I stood before Him empty handed. The fire of testing seemed to sweep away all of my religious doings. God did not want me to rest in these. For the future, I was to forget all that I might ever do for God, as quickly as it was accomplished, so that it might not prove a further snare to me, and go on as though I had never done a thing for God.... Satisfaction to self...must be shunned as we would a serpent" (*Azusa Street*, Frank Bartleman, Bridge Publishing, pg. 79.)

Yet God does use people in times of revival, particularly those who are hungry to be used. We are thrilled to see a reviving of a hunger to be fruitful in God's work. Those who are ignoring the outpouring of the Spirit and going on with their old agenda are not going to reap the automatic "bumper crop" they are hoping for. The best work at this moment in time will be tied in some way to revival. Charles Finney stated that a revival will cease whenever Christians get the idea that the work will go on without their aid.

When revival comes, either to your life individually or to your church, seek the Spirit's direction for every plan from that day forward. There are three vital ways we can cooperate and work with the Holy Spirit to promote revival:

SURRENDER your present program or lifestyle to God. Allow God to invade, **CHANGE** and rearrange whatever He desires. **FLOW** with whatever God is doing.

When the Holy Spirit first began to manifest in our services, we were unaccustomed to some of the behavior that began to surface. We were especially concerned when some took opportunity to interrupt the main speaker. Immediately we called a meeting of our leadership to bring things "back into order." But on the morning Pastor Paul was to instruct the people on this issue, a fear fell upon me. I knew Paul and I were treading on holy ground and I warned him to guard his words so that he did not impose more restraint upon the people than the Spirit wanted.

The power is God's, and we are but the vessels of impartation. So we hear, we go and we impart. What God is doing is so sacred, we have learned to walk into every service with great caution and sensitivity, almost as though we are in a mine field. Revival can flourish in this kind of reverent atmosphere.

Total Participation of the Body

Revivals will not flourish where there is negligence in the leadership or where there is sufficient resistance from the church body. Finney maintained, and rightly so, that God has been trying for 1,800 years "to get the Church into the work." This means the whole Church is to participate—the foot soldiers as well as the captains and generals.

Look at the world today. Satan worked on the leaders first, those who were steering the ships of education, government and the media. These leaders began to draw the United States of America away from God. But Satan did not stop there, he moved right on to his next goal—that every man, woman and child from kindergarten to the grave would undergo a moral reorientation and spiritual disorientation and surrender to his forces. The prince of this world is relentless in his recruitment of those who will help achieve this goal. Should the Church be less?

Every member of the Church should be set on fire with renewed zeal to go out into the world with the message of God. So why doesn't God just "fire up" His Church? Revival is initiated by the Spirit, the supernatural works are done by the Spirit, but the cooperation of man is essential. The Spirit is dispensing the fire of God to those who will receive it, but He will not force anyone to partake. Nor will He try to crowd His way into a heart choked with natural desires and anxieties.

Working closely with people as I do, I am continually reminded of the need for balance between the natural world and the spiritual kingdom of God that is increasingly pressing in upon it. Attitude seems to play a major role in walking wisely between our dual responsibilities in the natural and the supernatural realms. We are to remain in the world, dealing wisely with it and the natural responsibilities of our roles in life (businessman or woman, father or mother, boss or employee, etc.), yet always knowing that we are not "of the world."

Jesus made it clear that those who do not take care of their natural responsibilities should not expect God to impart spiritual responsibilities to them. "... *If you have not been faithful in the unrighteous mammon, who will commit to your trust the true riches?*" (Luke 16:11 NKJV). Since the revival began, we have had people come who wanted to enter into various ministries of the church. Yet, when it came to the everyday duties we all carry behind the scenes, they were found unfaithful. Such conduct immediately eliminated them from promotion to greater responsibility. Others came wanting prayer for financial miracles, yet they refused to work. Parents wanted prayer for unruly children who had been taught little about discipline. Young people wanted help from God while they lived in immoral relationships. The Bible tells us that when we have done what we know we should do righteously and morally, then we can expect God to move.

God has positioned the Church in this natural world, and the Church is made up of individuals who are encumbered by a host of natural responsibilities. However, Jesus clearly warned us about getting too engrossed in trying to secure a comfortable life in this present world:

> *"Do not lay up for yourselves treasures on earth, where moth and rust destroy and where thieves break in and steal; but lay up for yourselves treasures in heaven, where neither moth nor rust destroys and where thieves do not break in and steal. For where your treasure is, there your heart will be also."* (Matt. 6:19-21 NKJV)

People who allow themselves to be caught up in this present world, not spending time with God in personal prayer and immersion in the Word, always too busy to give themselves to the work of the Church or fellowship with other believers, are living unfruitful lives. As Jesus said, *"Where your treasure is, there will your heart be also."* The real test of our lives will be discovered through our heart, our motives, our hidden agendas—those desires that only God sees. Revival flourishes best in the midst of those who are willing to be examined and corrected by the Holy Spirit.

First Love

Revival is a time of recovering that fearless optimism that comes with "first love." First love gives itself wholly and without reservation to its lover. First love prefers to attend to the desires of its beloved more than its own needs. A woman called from out of state to say, "I have bought your book *'The Fresh Anointing'* and I'm so excited! I have given it to several pastors because I want to see these wonderful things happening all over New England!" And then the woman hesitated, "I hope I'm not getting carried away."

Afraid to believe that it was all right to give herself wholly to sharing understanding of God's outpouring! This is the state of much of the Church today—afraid to throw themselves completely into God's plans and purposes, afraid to be thought of as being too radical for God.

Finney warned that revival would always cease whenever the Church preferred to attend to selfish concerns rather than God's business. One greater than Finney said:

> *"Nevertheless I have this against you, that you have left your first love. Remember therefore from where you have fallen; repent and do the first works, or else I will come to you quickly and remove your lampstand from its place—unless you repent"* (Rev. 2:4 NKJV).

When exciting love is no longer in a marriage, the presence of the once-loved is no longer desirable or joyfully attended to. How many married people exist as though their partners were not around? When a Church in revival begins to get bored with the manifested presence of God, when they get weary at the demands of swimming in the river and want to return to just sitting on the river bank where it requires no energy—the revival flow will turn from that congregation and pour in the direction of dry riverbeds crying out for more water. One visitor even said to me one day, "I don't have the energy to come to your Church very often!" Yet I, who always had an energy shortage, am involved in every service, doing whatever the Holy Spirit instructs me to do, and new vitality continues to flow unceasingly into my life.

The Jonah Experience

A friend and I spent five days at a convention talking about the great revival we are entering into. On our way home, we were driving on the Garden State Parkway in New York when a tire went flat on our car. It was dark and the cars were whizzing by with such speed, we could feel the constant draft. Fortunately we had a phone in the car and soon help was on the way.

"Lord," I said to myself, "Surely this is not a divine appointment. We'll be blessed just to get out of here without being chopped to pieces with an ax." It so happened that a "good Samaritan" in Boston had recently stopped to help a supposed stranded motorist. As it turned out, it was a trap and the "good Samaritan" was brutally murdered by the very motorist he was trying to help. As we sat stranded on this New York thoroughfare at night, I immediately thought of this incident.

Approximately half an hour went by and a husky, young man with a heavy Italian accent pulled up. He went to work immediately, all the while assuring us that he understood our concern. When the job was finished, we asked him the cost. "I'll have to call my boss. It's after hours and I'm off duty," he said, dripping with perspiration. When the young man returned from making his call, to our surprise he said, "No charge. I'm offering my services free."

"No, I want to pay," I began to assure him.

"If I charge you, I must ask the price my boss quoted, which is too much. Just charge this one to me! I don't want to do anything dishonest."

"Do you like to read?" we inquired. When he said he loved to read, we asked, "Would you read something inspirational?"

"I surely would. I've been running from God all my life, but I recently stopped running!" Needless to say, I filled his hands with books I had written, to the point that he said, "No more! That's enough," as he turned to leave. With cars whizzing by and heavy gusts of wind distorting our voices, I clearly heard the young man call back, "Just remember when you pray to mention Christopher!"

It was a divine appointment after all. I had gone to this particular convention because I wanted to spread the news of the revival to the masses. But revival reaches people one at a time, whether they are driving a tow truck at night or sitting en masse. There are millions of Christophers waiting to hear that God is alive in this skeptical generation, and God will not hesitate to inconvenience us to see that they do. Revivals call for the "Jonah experience." Jonah didn't want to be inconvenienced for in order to bring revival to a pagan city. Rejecting that revival almost cost Jonah his life. Revival is God's idea not man's, and He does not take lightly those who ignore His plans. Jonah got smart and took the revival to Nineveh. The result was the saving of an entire population.

Is This Outpouring True Revival?

God has sent His Holy Spirit to bring refreshing, hope and power to the masses today, but is this outpouring a revival?   This is the question many continue to ask, especially in view of the unique manifestation of laughter accompanying today's outpouring. Yet "holy laughter" has accompanied spiritual awakenings since Abraham laughed and leaped over his promise of a son. Sarah laughed when that son was born, along with the whole camp, and she named this son of promise Isaac, meaning laughter.

While the Church continues to wring its hands and shake its head, the phenomena of laughter in the Church today is drawing the attention of the world around the globe. The August 1994 issue of TIME Magazine ran an article entitled *"Laughing for the Lord."* Featured was the Anglican Church in England where 1,500 people packed a standing room only service enjoying "hearty belly laughs." The February 1995 issue of NEWSWEEK carried the endorsement of the Archbishop of Canterbury for the continuing revival. And in March 1995, ABC television in the United States featured a one hour special on holy laughter entitled, "In the Name of God."

What does it all mean? That is what we are going to look at in the next chapter.

4

Laughter and More Laughter

"Recipe for holy laughter: Lie in prison for a few weeks. Hear the Lord turning the key. Follow him into the highroad. Your sky will burst with sunshine, and your heart with song and laughter" (*The Treasury of David*, Vol. III, Charles Spurgeon, MacDonald Publishing Co., McLean, VA 22102).

All we have to do is listen for the sound of His deliverance and then respond. Those who have ears, let them hear the voice of the Holy Spirit of God. He is again turning the key, just as He has in generations past. There is no new "laughter movement" beginning in the Church. What we are again hearing around the world is the joyous response to the sound of prison doors opening just as they have for centuries at the command of the King. Whenever those who have been barely existing with no hope and precious little strength are set free, they are often unable to contain their joyous relief. Gratitude and joy bubbles freely from deep within them.

No, God is not doing something new. He is just doing what He always does best—setting the captives free. *"When the Lord brought back the captivity of Zion, we were like them who dream. Then was our mouth filled with laughter...*" (Ps. 126:1,2 NKJV).

A minister from a large Congregational Church in New England phoned my office one day. After identifying herself, she said, "When I went home from the service at your church last week, I finally got to bed about 2:00 a.m. Thanksgiving began to flow out of me beginning with my childhood. It was as though God was showing me His hand upon my entire life. What a joy!" Then she made a very perceptive statement about the body of Christ: "The Church has long leaned heavily on contemporary therapy to help heal the inner wounds of people. It's good to identify our hurting areas, but that doesn't go far enough. What we really need to learn is to identify Christ."

Revival is a time to identify Christ. It is a time when God lifts His people above their present "cares and pleasures" and helps them to rediscover the very real joys of knowing Him. The minister who made this insightful statement had just enjoyed such a time, a wonderful evening of laughter and worship in the manifested presence of God's Spirit. The touch of God literally awakened strains of her life all the way back to childhood, not with regret, but with great pleasure.

Paying or Praying for Laughter?

What price is man willing to pay for the pleasure of laughter? The world's masses pay comedians millions of dollars a year to make them laugh. Performers who can make people laugh consistently are not only paid exorbitant salaries, but they are rewarded with fame, adulation and the label of "greatness." People will travel long distances and purchase expensive tickets to hear them. It is ironic that great evil as well as great good has been transacted through the vehicle of laughter in every field of communication.

Laughter is pleasurable, but it is much more powerful than simple pleasure. The Bible tells us that laughter is physically beneficial. *"A merry heart doeth good like a medicine ..."* (Prov. 17:22 KJV). Medicine is the most effective when it is taken in regular doses by those who will admit they need it. We are a generation of bound-up people who could benefit greatly from some regular trips to God's medicine chest. We've lost our ability to laugh.

Laughter was given to man to glorify God. The liberated captives of ancient Judah said of their release, *"When the Lord turned again the captivity of Zion, we were like them that dream."* This verse should actually be translated, "We were like unto those restored to health." The Hebrew words used here suggest recovery or restoration of health. To the returning captives from Babylon, God's deliverance was like a dream finally realized.

When God sets us free, it is like recovering from a long illness. It seems almost too good to be true. Many who have come into the glorious services we are now enjoying at Christian Teaching and Worship Center tell us something wonderful God has done for them and then they hesitantly ask, "Is this really real? Is it true?"

Why are so many almost afraid to believe in what God is bestowing upon them through the miracle of joy and laughter? This is certainly a negative testament to the bondage we have permitted in the Church because the body of Christ has ceased to identify its first love. There is such tremendous joy in identifying Christ, a joy that heals and sets free.

How can some sit in wonderful services where the Holy Spirit is pouring out joy and freedom, actually sitting right beside others who have been healed and set free, and then say, "Well, I liked many things about the service, but I don't know about the laughter"? Several books and articles already on the market, as well as some well-known Christian radio shows, are decrying the demonstrations of joy within churches. I am repeatedly reading or hearing people say, "God is definitely moving, but I don't think the laughter is from Him." Let me apply some very practical logic to this kind of reasoning:

If we are willing to admit that God is definitely moving in these services where people are laughing, then surely He must not be offended. And if God is not offended, why should we be?

The Test of Time

Five years ago there was no significant laughter (that we knew of!) going on in the Church anywhere in the world. Now, all of a sudden, holy laughter is happening on every continent. People's lives are changing as their bodies, souls and spirits are being healed. If this joy and laughter is not coming from God, then where is it coming from? I certainly can think of nothing in today's natural circumstances of worldwide crime, murder, starvation, poverty, disease and war that is fostering such delight.

Sufficient time has now passed to begin to evaluate some of the changes resulting from the fresh anointing that many churches have experienced and still are. The laughter continues to flow in our services in varying degrees. Sometimes there is very little laughter and the service takes a totally different tone. At other times, the laughter may continue for as much as one or more hours during the service.

This infectious joy has not been limited to meetings within our church. Some of the young families of our congregation get together for a meal and fellowship only to end up laughing uncontrollably. Women call each other on the phone during the week only to have laughter break out for several minutes.

Is this only foolishness? I believe these are better questions: Is it more beneficial for young mothers to discuss their troubles and woes or to fill their souls with laughter? Does it make more sense to take tranquilizers, pay thousands of dollars a year for a therapist, abuse credit cards and have frustration fights with your spouse or to call a friend and have a refreshing of good laughter in the presence of the Spirit of the Lord?

In one service, a woman stood before me with a blanket of depression completely covering her sorrowful face and sagging shoulders. The veil over her eyes and the weight on her shoulders spoke volumes, and I hardly needed to ask, "What do you want Jesus to do for you?" to know she was oppressed by fear and depression. When she said she knew the Lord, I asked, "Well, do you worship, sing, clap your hands, leap, shout, dance, laugh and celebrate before Him?" Hesitatingly she said that she only sang before Him.

"Well, singing is obviously not enough for you to break out of this depression! That is why God has given you many weapons to fight the enemy of your mind," I assured her as I began to pray. When I finished, I took her by the hand and ran down the aisle of the church, praising and laughing before God. "Use all your weapons! Depression will not stay where leaping and shouting before God are continually practiced!"

Does this just sound like emotionalism to you? If you are thinking yes, then you haven't read the latest in psychiatric medicine! The healing systems of the world seem more aware of the power of laughter than the Church. Laughter has been breaking out in churches all over the world, yet the Church itself seems severely constricted over the subject and much controversy has ensued. Many pastors, upon seeing congregations rolling with laughter, have said, "Revival is just around the corner, but this is not it!"

I implore these men and women of God to be very cautious in making such a judgment! Consider some of the recent findings from the unbelieving world. The September 1994 issue of "Virtue" magazine featured an article entitled *"The Funny Bone Factor!"* According to documented research done at the Gelotolgy Institute of Stanford University Medical School (the science of mirth) under Dr. William Fry, laughing turns the body into a human vibrator that massages practically every internal organ. It has also been proven that laughing strengthens the immune system, lightens pain, eases stress and improves circulation and breathing. According to this article, even so much as a chuckle:

- Stimulates your endocrine system to lower hormones that arouse high-frequency alertness.
- Triggers secretions that speed up metabolism and aid digestion.
- Signals production of immunoglobulin, believed to mobilize defenses against infection.
- Creates more fast-wave alpha activity in the right hemisphere of your brain (the emotional, creative half) than the logical, censorious left.

The author of this article dared to say, "Go ahead and laugh out loud! Double over and roll on the floor." I have not heard anyone criticizing this doctor as a radical. Yet when ministers state that God is sending laughter to the Church and people's attitudes and health are changing, they are considered heretical, unholy and radical. God knew, long before Stanford University did, that laughter is health to the soul and body. And He is sending it to His people without expensive research!

Taking God for Granted

The Church is guilty of taking the things of God for granted. Few of us would argue with Stanford Medical School, but most of us argue (at least initially) with laughter in our church services. Because He didn't send along a medical explanation, scientific documentation and celebrity verification to relieve us of having to exercise our faith, God's good work has been called everything from radical to heresy. Several pastors have made the statement, "I know God has revival for my congregation, but He has told us it will come in His timing." (Translation: "I do not agree with what is happening in the Church today under the label of revival, and I am going to wait for something that I find more palatable.") Well, revival is not going to come their way. It is already here and it has come God's way!

God has always made it clear that He is not in the business of sending "tailor-made" revivals. That which is yet "coming" is simply going to be more of what has already arrived. Those who do not like what they are seeing now are not going to not like what is to follow, for this refreshing is going to come only one way—God's way. God is not going to modify His vehicle of revival, His holy laughter, for the benefit of human logic. But, if I may be "logical" about the obvious: If natural laughter has such curative ability for the body, what must Spirit-initiated laughter be doing for the whole person?

I walked back among the people during one worship service when the laughter was rolling in like waves of an ocean. Joy was thick and tangible all over the sanctuary. A couple was seated at the end of an aisle near the back, and the expression on both their faces was hard and angry. My eyes suddenly locked with theirs. We held our stare for a moment, and then I turned and started back down the aisle without speaking a word. As I neared the front, I turned to look back at the couple once more only to find two empty chairs. The impact of the challenge in that place was more than they could bear. I'm sure they felt they had escaped from foolishness, but my heart was grieved for their imprisonment in their own rigid form.

This holy laughter changes those who receive it, and it challenges those who won't. The Spirit has come to set the captives free. The One with the key has arrived to unlock the gate that will allow the spirit man to spring forth. Will we remain locked inside because we do not like the style of the key?

Three Levels of Laughter

Laughter is a God-designed part of the human make-up. It has purpose as surely as the heart is designed to pump blood. There are actually three levels of laughter in which human beings engage. One is natural, two are supernatural.

One

There is a natural laughter that I call "one of nature's tranquilizers." This occurs when friends or family get together and healthy wholesome conversation recalls pleasant experiences. Natural laughter is a device built into all humans that gives us pleasure and helps to maintain a healthy attitude toward life. Natural laughter is under the control of the mind. This is the laughter Stanford University Medical school is researching. Wisely used, it helps to relieve a lot of tension in the everyday stresses of life, and it improves the mind's evaluation of situations.

Two

There is a supernatural level of laughter that Satan controls. Knowing the nature of God, *"He that sits in the heavens shall laugh,"* and knowing the nature of God's creatures, Satan has tapped into one of the most powerful aspects of the human life. Through man's natural need of and delight in laughter, Satan has enticed "fallen human nature" into every base act of immorality imaginable! For proof, one only needs to observe the thousands of movies and television plots using laughter to deliver ungodly messages. People are literally laughing all the way to personal disaster.

It seems that Satan knows the power of laughter better than the people of God! His use of laughter in the past thirty years in the Western world is supernaturally clever. Through the world's comedy—drugs, immorality, homosexuality, lying, adultery, gambling, stealing and violence have been made to seem both amusing and "normal." Laughing is being used to desensitize us to the real nature and consequences of our sins. It has been a major tool in helping to lull society into the spirit of the New Age. We laugh about sin, we laugh about Satan, we laugh about sacred things. And the more we laugh with Satan, the deeper we sink.

Three

There is a laughter from the throne of God that is sparked by victory. *"He who sits in the heavens shall laugh; the Lord shall have them [His enemies] in derision"* (Ps. 2:4 NKJV). Holy laughter in the Church is evidence that God is pushing back the enemy. A church that is rising up from defeat will laugh. A church that is being released from prison will laugh. A church that is drinking new wine will laugh.

> "If the heart be glad, the tongue is glib. Joy cannot be suppressed in the heart, but it must be expressed with the tongue," quoted Spurgeon in his argument for joy (ibid., 74).

From the same writings, Martin Luther is quoted as saying of the Scripture, *"Then was our mouth filled with laughter...."*:

> "We must earnestly endeavor to learn this practice (laughter)...And we must raise up ourselves with this consideration: That the gospel is nothing else but laughter and joy" (ibid., 74).

The Witness of Godly Laughter

> *"When the Lord turned again the captivity of Zion, we were like them that dream. Then was our mouth filled with laughter, and our tongue with singing: then said they [the world] among the heathen, The Lord hath done great things for them"* (Ps. 126:1,2 KJV).

The unbelieving world takes note of the laughter of believers and it shakes them to see the godly laughing. TIME Magazine, August 1994, contained an article, *"Laughing for the Lord,"* with a caption that read:

> **"Revivalist fervor has invaded the Church of England!"** (The article then described worshipers falling to

the floor with) "...hands twitching....Within an hour there are bodies everywhere as supplicants sob, shake, roar like lions and strangest of all, laugh uncontrollably.... Lines outside Holy Trinity now start forming an hour and a half before services.... Laughing revivals have been reported in Anglican parishes from Manchester to York to Brighton."

What the reporter did not know was that it had spread also into the Baptist, free churches and Assembly of God as well. Right before our eyes, the close of the twentieth century is showing God's word being confirmed: *"And I will shew signs in the earth..."* (Acts 2:19 KJV). But as Spurgeon quoted of the laughing captives of Judah:

> "...It is a pity the 'heathen' said it, and that the Jews themselves spake not these words first. But now, finding the 'heathen' so saying, and it was all true...They must needs find themselves bound to say at least as much."

What a shame that Stanford University School of Medicine and TIME Magazine publish the value of laughing at a time when many in the Church are still wondering about—or worse yet, trying to quench and discredit—joyous laughter in the Church as revival from the Spirit. What a shame if we should drag our feet until revival becomes so obvious that the man on the street knows more about it than the Church. Faith will have no opportunity then, and the joys of being a front-runner will have passed in skepticism. Oh, to be among the first to have our mouths filled with the joyful breath of Him who sits in the heavens—laughing.

Waiting For What?

Shall we wait to see what others will say? God has spoken and that is sufficient. We at the Christian Teaching and Worship Center are laughing! And the results of this joyous freedom are literally pouring in. We have finally become a great team of witnesses. Without any evangelistic program, people who have never told anyone about Christ are now bringing them in, to the extent that we are having to knock down the walls to accommodate the people. Hearts are changing, bodies are being healed, lives are being restored, and joy is breaking out in epidemic proportion.

A father and his two sons stopped by our bookstore one day, and I happened to notice them and took a moment to introduce myself. The father said, "We're looking for material that will describe to the boys what you believe and teach at this church. We visited here for the first time last week, and we just loved it. But coming from a very traditional background, I'm not sure how to explain what is taking place." Then the man related an observation his eight-year old made after their first visit. "As we talked about what we had experienced on the way home last week, my youngest son said, 'Dad I know God is in that place, you can see it in the people's eyes!'"

And exactly what is *it*? It is joy! What the young boy saw in our eyes was the joy of the Lord being released from souls filled with God's presence in our midst—waves and waves of joy that are setting God's people free!

A couple in our congregation, well known in the Boston area for their successful air freight company, took a "wait and see" position toward the revival. Almost ten months went by and they were still waiting. One evening the laughter hit this reserved couple. "I feel ten years younger," the woman confessed recently. "I've never been happier or felt better. Even with the added pressures of the business, I don't worry anymore."

Laughter in the Church, laughter in the business world, laughter in the scientific world. Do you know that scientists have discovered "laughing gas" in the far reaches of our galaxy? The discovery came as a result of their celestial search for the building blocks of life, according to Lewis Snyder, an astrophysicist at the University of Illinois in Urbana. Who knows, perhaps the whole heavens are enjoying the laughter of God. Job said the stars sing, why wouldn't they also laugh?

An atheist was invited to our revival services by a friend. Educated and skeptical, he observed the laughter and joyous celebration. After two or three visits, the atheist made a very insightful statement: "I do not believe there is a God, but if I did, what is going on here makes perfect sense." Laughter, joy and rejoicing do "make sense" when you have been rescued from the death penalty, have eternal life and are loved by the God who created all things.

Saved and loved is far more cause to celebrate than to see someone throw a round ball through a hoop or kick it through posts. The atheist came forward for prayer three weeks later.

5

Can Men Stop Revival?

God is doing something special in the earth today. Before it is over, both the Church and the world will acknowledge its impact. It is called revival. Revival begins with seed corn. From His spiritual granary, God takes a handful of His Spirit and casts it out over the earth. The wise take the "revival seeds" and plant them—watering, digging and nurturing the revival until the harvest comes.

In this hour we are being given "revival seed." Yet, to a certain extent, the measure of the harvest will depend on the amount of effort we put into cultivating that seed. The blind will ignore the rains. The slumbering will refresh themselves. Only the hungry will plant and work the fields until the "gusher" arrives, that all who are thirsty may be refreshed.

According to Charles Finney:

1) "A revival will stop if the Church believes it is going to cease." (Don't meditate on when the revival will cease.)

2) "A revival will cease when Christians consent that it should cease." (Negative comments and

> growing indifference must be weeded out regularly.)

3) "A revival will cease whenever Christians become mechanical in their attempts to promote it." (Water your own personal revival and keep it real with worship.)

4) "A revival will cease whenever Christians get the idea that the work will go on without their aid." (Renew your zeal through testimony and fellowship with those in revival.)

5) "A revival will cease when the Church prefers to attend to selfish concerns rather than God's business." (Guard your time. Give God's things generous attention.)

In this chapter, we are going to conclude Finney's list of reasons (all references to Charles Finney's sayings in this chapter can be found in *Revivals of Religion*, Charles G. Finney, CBN University Press) why revival fires become smoking embers. Surely nothing is more grievous to God's heart than to pour out His Spirit upon parched souls only to have them drink for themselves alone and produce nothing for others who are dying from thirst.

Tending the Revival

Spending my first years on a farm, I learned early how to identify poor soil. Poor soil drinks in the rains but brings no fruit to maturity. When God sends revival into an individual's life, or a church body, He is not seeking to just bless them personally. God wants fruit to come forth.

We will always want fruit, too, when we understand that an unproductive life is a most miserable existence. We enjoy a true and lasting sense of satisfaction only as we are productive. God is glorified and we are satisfied only with "much fruit." *"Herein is my Father glorified that ye bear much fruit. . .,"* Jesus said in John 15:8 (KJV). So when the Spirit comes, He comes looking for fruit. Revival is God's fruit-bearing season.

The Church needs to get ready, for we're about to give birth to some great works. These will be works of such magnitude, pride will have to be dealt with promptly. This is, in fact, Finney's next warning:

> 6) "Where Christians get proud of their 'great revival,' it will cease."

The pride suggested here is one where those who are carrying the work begin to compare themselves with others, developing an attitude of superiority. After eight months of continual revival, I had occasion to be alone in another city. Near the hotel where I was staying was a large, well-known church. On Sunday morning I slipped into an aisle seat where it didn't take long to see that the fresh anointing had not invaded them. Yet, as the service unfolded, I saw that a kind and generous attitude had been planted by that minister into his people. They were involved in many fine works throughout the world and enthusiastic about yet another project being laid before them.

After the service was over I met the pastor and his wife and gave them a copy of my book about the revival, with a brief explanation. I also congratulated them on the work they are doing. When I returned to my room at the hotel, God dealt with me about the dangers of developing a wrong, pride-based attitude about revival. When the fire of God falls, it separates and divides. There can be no revival without division. As much as we would like to maintain a safe comfort zone among fellow believers, change shows. Yet, this "change" can be exhibited with humility or with pride.

I went home immediately and warned our church against the wrong attitude. With humility we are being invited by the Holy God to *"go out with joy, and be led forth out with peace; . . ."* (Isa. 55:12 NAS). One minister called us recently, a call that took tremendous humility, for initially he had been unresponsive to our ovations concerning revival. He asked, "Will you come to my church and share with us about what's going on? I think we need it."

He was right, of course. God would not be sending revival if we did not all need it! How wonderful to be humble before our most considerate and patient God. And God is considerate, as Finney points out in his next statement:

7) "The revival will stop when the Church gets exhausted by labor."

Finney was cautioning us that excitement can push people to overdo their role in the work. This was one of the first areas of concern we encountered, for revivals are not sent to wear out bodies or break up families. How would we be able to hold three- and four-hour services three times a week and sometimes even more? In truth, we are managing quite well with a few occasional adjustments.

For one thing, the great burden of trying to "make something happen" that will affect people's lives has been lifted from our church leadership. God has assumed the responsibility for changing hearts and circumstances quite successfully with a supernatural anointing. Secondly, we are personally being refreshed in a remarkable way as the anointing of the Spirit has an invigorating effect upon the human body. There is literal energy in the presence of God.

A former member of our congregation came for a visit when she heard of the revival. The statement she kept repeating was one most of us have heard individually, "Everybody looks so healthy, so young!" Joy is indeed restorative. As a person who has dealt with a life-long energy deficit, I can testify to the fact that I am being sustained by the life that is in this revival. A good portion of that energy emanates from the laughter that is bubbling out of our spirits during worship and praise. One young mother reported that her family of "non-participants" are baffled at her changed countenance. "Even your eyes look brighter and your skin clearer," they said in amazement.

Yet, we continue to remain sensitive to the fact that we live in human bodies that must, without being pampered, be respected. This has prompted us to limit the amount of entertaining we do beyond the services. Our family's first response to the revival was to invite the world to come, trying to house and feed every visitor who responded. Wisdom has taught us that we are feeding them by continually giving ourselves to revival. We cannot also try to be a host in natural matters, not if we want to last the duration of this outpouring! Since our entire family is in ministry, we have set aside Sunday afternoon as a time to get together and give our attention to the children of the family and to each other. We are all blessed with a good sense of humor and we unwind the week's work with a lot of natural laughter on family matters. This plan works for us.

Simplicity is a gift from God. A Christianity that does not affect the everyday affairs of man is useless. Finney pointed out this very danger in his next point:

8) "A revival will cease when the Church begins to speculate about abstract doctrines, which have nothing to do with practice."

A valuable lesson this revival has taught Paul and me is the difference between a worship service and a classroom, textbook analysis of Scripture. As founders of Kaleo Bible Institute, Paul and I love to do exegetical research of word and text meanings. And, of course, there is a need and a place for academic scriptural research. Such study helps to maintain clarity and purity of basic beliefs (excluding skeptic professors whose primary intention is to discredit the Word). A worship service is not a classroom. Worship is man's lifeline to God. A worship service is a time when God calls His family around Him in order to touch their lives, to allow them to commune and fellowship with Him in the presence of other family members.

In worship, there is community music, praises, celebration, prayers, and words of encouraging prophecy and exhortation. The Holy Spirit is present for the purpose of lifting oppressive burdens. He is there to heal and bring spiritual enlightenment, as well as give instruction from the Word. In worship there is a corporate anointing unlike any other experience with God. A genuine revival seems to lift those experiencing it above the Church's doctrinal pursuits and differences. Genuine revival brings the bigger picture into light, and it tends to focus the attention back on God himself. If doctrinal "hair splitting" is to be imposed upon the worship service of a people in revival, it will kill the restorative spirit that prevails.

I am not sure I can explain what has happened to my teaching since the revival came. I have always done extensive research and strived to pour out the most scriptural understanding and rich insight into the Word I could possibly give. Now, the revival seems to have shifted me slightly away from so much expounding upon and more toward experiencing the God of the Word that I am teaching from. I often feel as though I and the congregation are walking around inside the Word as I am speaking. The Word is much nearer to us, more attainable, more a part of us than before.

In the case of one dramatic healing during a service, the healed woman said, "If you had not preached that message tonight, I was going to speak it. When you talked about the power of God to do the impossible, it was a message burning in my heart." What happened to the woman is obvious: She had entered into the Word even before the prayer for her condition had been offered. She was already walking around in the life of the Word!

Academic Stillborns

Seminaries, in their lofty pursuit of mental excellence and textbook accuracy, often obscure the real purpose of what they have been raised up to do. IBM produces computers capable of retaining massive amounts of textual, mathematical and graphic information that can be retrieved at will. This is their stated purpose. Seminaries and Bible training centers have a responsibility to impart much information, but unlike IBM, these instructors are handling living words that have the ability to affect lives as nothing else on earth can do. Unless the teachers and mentors in these biblical institutions learn to take their information from the textbooks into their hearts in such a way that the

Word accomplishes its divine purpose, they will not be able to impart life into the hearts of their students. Neither the teachers or the students will ever achieve their highest purpose with pure academic scholarship alone.

The purpose of seminaries and Bible teaching institutions must always be to impart living words and living truths in such a way that those who have thus received will then be able to pass that life on to others. Bible-training institutions that do not pass on this life, and the ability to reproduce it in others, graduate "academic stillborns." Most of those stillborns end up in a pulpit speaking with little, if any, life-changing impact. This defeats God's purpose. Jesus said, *"I have come that they [you] might have life, and that they [you] might have it more abundantly"* (John 10:10 KJV). Life is **the divine** *product the Church is to impart.* Life is what seminaries and Bible institutes are supposed to be all about.

Revivals bring life and they belong in every institution that names the name of Christ. This includes the Christian media of television, radio and literature. It is the life flow of Jesus Christ within a man or woman that gives them boldness to take courageous stands for righteousness in the face of great peril.

The day of hiding behind Gamaliel's "middle-of-the-road safe stand" is over. When the question of the disciples of Jesus came up among the Sanhedrin, Gamaliel wisely instructed them, *". . .For if this counsel or this work be of men, it will come to nought: but if it be of God, ye cannot overthrow it: lest haply ye be found even to fight against God"* (Acts 5:38,39 KJV). Gamaliel was not a follower of Christ and therefore would not take a stand for His disciples, but he knew enough to fear crossing that which might be sacred.

For a Christian to take no position when the Spirit of revival is being poured out is unwarranted ignorance. If we do not know what position to take, then we have a responsibility to search until we do know. There is always a point where "waiting to see" becomes rebellion and laziness. Revival is for human beings, not for God: How can there be any revival if every human being just "waits to see?"

Proof of Revival and New Life

Many have said this revival is not of God. But since it came to our church:

1) People are being saved.
2) Love and concern for one another has blossomed.
3) Children and young people are excited about Jesus.
4) Peoples' lives are being restored.
5) Bodies are being healed.
6) God is being glorified and worshiped.
7) We have experienced wonderful numerical growth.

And this has continued since November 1993! What more proof of a genuine revival by the Holy Spirit does anyone need? As one person said, "I love Jesus more than I've ever loved Him before. If this is Satan, then someone please explain. Are we to believe we are being so blessed by the devil?"

The spirit of the New Age movement has kissed the Church and believers are being romanced to accept whatever appears to bring happiness and peace. The saying that "he who believes all things believes nothing" still holds true. Christianity not only requires private faith, it demands public proclamation. The world is hungry for the light of someone who will take a clear and concise stand on divisive and seemingly confusing issues of life.

Revivals are looking for people who will commit and not back down when the heat pours in. Jesus made it clear in His greatest of all parables, that the seed of truth falls on four types of soil (Matt. 13), but it flourishes only on one. The four types are:

1) Those who receive because it sounds exciting but soon fall away because it was only an emotional response.
2) Those who receive but give up when their friends and family object.
3) Those who receive but are so busy with the problems and pleasures of their life, they "don't have time."
4) Those who receive and commit to God's way all the way and produce a return harvest one-hundred fold.

In spite of those who are resisting the present outpouring, there are many who have made "all-the-way" commitments to God's way of revival. We're never surprised anymore at who God brings to us. One Jewish man walked into our building during business hours saying, "I've got to settle this issue of Messiah." He was met by our youth pastor who prayed with him to receive Jesus as Messiah. Without one word of explanation or prompting, the man then began speaking in tongues. He later said, "I'd never even heard about this, but the words just came bubbling out!"

A young Vietnamese woman received a call from a relative in California. "Go to Christian Teaching and

Worship Center in Boston. We read in Charisma that they are in revival." The young woman came, desperately desiring to be touched by God. She was gloriously filled with the Holy Spirit and set free to worship in great liberty. "I never thought it would happen to me!" she cried.

A Jewish evangelist from Israel saw the book *"The Fresh Anointing"* on display and drawn to the book, he took it to his hotel and read it at 2:00 in the morning. He then came and told us, "This confirms everything my heart has been crying out for!"

One couple in ministry, who had strongly opposed the message of *"The Fresh Anointing,"* were sent a revival tape by our church. When our son went to collect the tape, the husband and wife were stretched out on the floor—laughing. They began spreading this joy in the former Soviet Union where they were working.

Other cultures and races, other denominations and backgrounds—they've been coming. A couple from Nigeria came to one of our services. Through a word of knowledge, I called for someone present who was desperate to have a child. This man and his wife came forward, and we laid hands on them and prayed. This week we dedicated their new baby with this glorious testimony: "For thirteen-and-a-half years, we have prayed and sought medical help for a child. After my wife was prayed for, she became pregnant. A few weeks later, the doctor examined her blood stream and said, 'This is a bad pregnancy.' But we maintained confidence in the integrity of God that *'He who had begun a good work would also perform it'* (Phil. 1:6 paraphrased). Today, we celebrate the faithfulness of our God manifest in the life of Osarim!"

During a service one morning our head usher came into the sanctuary and motioned for one of our altar ministers. Kathy went out into the hallway and found a young man in tears. "I met the Lord sixteen years ago, but I've strayed away. I want to be restored to God," he pleaded. Holding tightly to Kathy's hands, his tears soaked the cuffs of her blouse sleeves. "I saw your service on television, and even though my wife is strongly opposed, I've got to get my life straightened out with God!" This type of conviction does not come from a television broadcast or from the persuasiveness of a dynamic minister. Such an acknowledgment of spiritual need comes only from the working of the Spirit of God as He draws hearts to himself, irregardless of their religious orientation—which brings us to Finney's next point:

> 9) "Revivals will decline when Christians begin to proselytize."

Webster's Dictionary defines proselytizing as: To convert from one religion, belief or party to another; to recruit members especially by the offer of special inducements. As soon as other churches heard about the revival at our church, people began to come. Some were discontented where they were, some were simply hungry to be touched by God. God recently spoke through prophecy during one of our services, "Don't ever leave your church because of trouble. Go to your pastor and reconcile the grievance. When you have made peace in so far as it is possible, then you may with clear conscience make your choice." Our ministers have been duly cautioned about saying anything that would pull someone away from his or her own church. "Get touched, go back and be a blessing!" we encourage all who come from other bodies of believers.

Over the years, we have found that the majority of people who leave a church under poor circumstances rarely stay with the next church either. This is not to say that people should remain in a dead church because of family tradition. But every effort should be made to reconcile differences, clear consciences and then, if a desire to depart is still in the heart, consider leaving. One family began coming to our church and they loved what they found. After several months, they went to their pastor who was from a strict liturgical order and said to him, "We love you, but we are hungry for more of God and we have found a place where we are getting fed." He blessed them and they parted on good terms. Not always will pastors bless such a decision, but if their hearts are pure in the matter I believe God will bless the change.

> 10) "Revivals decline when Christians refuse to render to the Lord according to the benefits received."

Revivals are times when the windows of heaven have been opened and God generously bestows His gifts and blessings during times of spiritual refreshings. In return, He expects His people to become liberal in their giving of themselves, too. *"Freely you have received, [now] freely give,"* Jesus reminds us in Matthew 10:8 (KJV). God is generous. He not only gave the best of heaven to man—Jesus, He is still giving daily by His Spirit. Revival stirs up man's desire to give. When revival came to our church, our people spontaneously became more generous. They are increasingly liberal with their money, their time and their talents in ways they never expressed before.

Can man stop revival? According to Mr. Finney, the work may be hindered:

> 11) "When Christians do not feel their dependence on the Spirit,"
>
>   a) by beginning to seek self-glory,
>   b) by speaking lightly of the revival—overstating or exaggerating.
>
> 12) "When they lose the spirit of brotherly love."

Mr. Finney said he never saw nor heard of a revival where brotherly love did not flourish. This has certainly been true in our experience. Both forgiveness and compassion have both risen to the top like cream. We have seen some chronic personality clashes become totally healed—others are learning to stretch their tolerance. As one member put it, "I no longer tolerate people, I actually like them." Another member called me one day and said, "Since the revival, I see that you are actually just like the rest of us. I really like you!"

We not only find that we really like each other, I see an integration taking place among the various nationalities as well as a sweet attitude toward the mentally-disturbed segment of our society that the church has never really addressed. Troubled people who come into our worship services are embraced and encouraged in the same manner as anyone else. God commands us to comfort the "feeble minded," so we do. And what a great feeling it brings in return!

People are beginning spontaneously to open their homes and invite people in for fellowship. One Sunday evening, about ten o'clock, our "Joy Minister" called, and we could hear the celebration going on in the background. "It's great over here!" she said, laughing freely. "Twenty six people are crammed into this small apartment and you can hear the rejoicing all the way down the street."

It reminded me of something I used to hear when I was growing up in the South. Many times, as the adults sat around talking, I would hear them refer to the post-Azusa Street days "when you could walk by a farm house in the evening and hear people praying or shouting." Those were days when no one locked his doors or feared to walk the roads and streets of America. It is a spiritual and moral posture that America would do well to return to—which brings us to a most unusual statement made by Mr. Finney concerning revival:

> 13) "A revival will decline and cease, unless Christians are frequently reconverted."

This may seem the strangest of all Finney's statements, but once I read it, I immediately understood something that was occurring in our revival that had concerned me. After a few months into the revival, I noticed that the same "core" kept coming back for more and more of the anointing. Our daughter Susan and I were among them. Susan has received an intoxicating laughter which she frequently breaks out into during worship. Sometimes I break out in laughter. At other times I fall to the floor where God gives me a wonderful truth to share with the people. Quite often I feel intoxicated, light and joyful after these experiences.

What about those of us who continue to repeat our experiences, over and over? I can affirm that it is only setting me more free and restoring many things within and without my life. But does that make it right? This was my recurring question until I read Mr. Finney's statement that "a revival will decline and cease, unless Christians are frequently reconverted." He then went on to clarify his statement by saying:

> "By this I mean that Christians, in order to keep in the spirit of revival, commonly need to be frequently convicted, and humbled and broken down before God. . ." (ibid., 298).

Then I understood. We need to be continually resubmerged into the flow if we will remain in the spirit of a revival. No person who takes one swallow of alcohol comes under its control. To be "filled" with the Spirit, as the Book of Acts describes the first believers, means "to come under the control of." The more we participate in revival, the more we come under the control of it. The more we drink of the Spirit, the more we surrender our will to His power. The more we drink of the presence of God, the more we desire to be purged of our sins and selfishness and the more God takes over our lives. This should serve as an encouragement to anyone who feels guilty about always entering into the flow of the Spirit during a worship service. When the Spirit starts to flow, let the thirsty come and drink. There is such a thing as too much religion, but no one has too much of God.

One young mother in our church had lost her mother when she was young, and she had to assume adult family responsibilities at an early age. This mother of three felt she had missed a big portion of her teen years. Since our revival, she has entered into a most refreshing laughter that breaks out just about anywhere. She now says, "I feel better and younger than I have ever felt in my entire life! I feel light and free." This is revival. It is the "times of refreshing from the presence of the Lord," promised to God's people. It is life from the purest stream.

Can men stop revival? Mr. Finney closed with the remaining check list. I believe it is a list every pastor should attach to his office door so that he reviews it frequently. It is for churches, but it applies to each of us individually as well.

- Practice self denial.
- Avoid controversies about the new changes.
- Don't ignore social conditions. Do not neglect missions.
- Avoid slandering revivals.
- Do not bow down to the censorship of complainers.
- Do not neglect to educate young people for the ministry.

Educating People for the Ministry

Several years ago, God placed a desire in our hearts for a quality Bible institute. We began a journey in that direction with special evening courses. In 1991, we opened Kaleo Bible Institute—a full-time diploma program that is already at provisional status for accreditation. Oral Roberts University is extending themselves greatly in this endeavor to strengthen and upgrade the standards of new Bible institutions that are being birthed worldwide.

Now that revival has come, I understand the birthing of such schools. Bible schools have almost become extinct in America. According to our investigation, I think the whole of New England (with its millions of people) has only two fully-accredited "Christian" colleges. Even the best of these two admitted that they were more secular than biblical. So, once again God is raising up sound Bible-training institutions that are taught by believers. In order for a revival to have maximum effect, Bible training institutions must also be revived or they will uproot large portions of what the Holy Spirit imparts. Of the ninety-seven greatest colleges and universities in New England, ninety-two of them were originally founded by the Church. Revival is a time when the sacred call to knowledge is purged and the **purpose** of knowledge is refocused back on knowing God and living life by His principles.

Seminaries, departments of theology and Bible colleges are set to have an encounter with God. Those that enter in will be revitalized and used by God in this hour. Those that eliminate themselves will become twice dead as they feed on self. Charles Finney said of education:

> "A minister may be very learned and yet not wise.... A minister may be very wise, though he is not learned.... A learned minister, and a wise minister, are two different things. Facts in the history of the Church in all ages prove this. It is very common for churches, when looking for a minister, to aim at getting a very learned man. Do not understand me to discourage learning. The more learning the better, if he is also wise in the great matter he is employed about. If a minister knows how to win souls, the more learning he has the better.... Those are the best educated ministers who win the most souls."

I go back to the observation made by modern physicist Stephen Hawking, "Knowledge has done nothing to stop humanity's caveman instinct toward self-destruction." There is a wisdom (knowledge and wisdom are not synonymous!), however, that can lift us out of our destiny with annihilation and set us among princes. The purpose of instructing the unlearned in the Word of God is not to raise up institutions for amassing knowledge. The purpose is this: *These things are written that you may believe that Jesus is the Christ, the Son of God, and that believing you may have life through his name"* (John 20:31 NKJV).

Institutions of biblical learning exist that men might find life in Jesus Christ. This is the accreditation God requires.

6

A Divine Encounter

A genuine revival from God does not just bring a blessed, comfortable little "spiritual stirring" in the pews. Refreshings from the presence of the Lord awaken people from spiritual slumber, purifying and empowering their lives for God's use. True revivals are a time when the Spirit calls those inside the Church to His true purposes. Great harvesting of the lost souls of the world can only be the result of a genuine revival first within the Church.

The works of God are carried on by people He has set apart, sanctified, to do them. The word "sanctified" in the New Testament comes from the original Greek word *hagiasmos* (holy) meaning consecration, a separation from a secular carnal use to a sacred spiritual use. It is possible to avoid the commission of "moral" sins of the flesh and still sin by the omission of never answering God's call to serve Him. The sanctified life not only avoids sin, but it sets aside even "good" things when called upon to do works for the sake of the Gospel.

Holiness brings about separation. By definition, the basic idea of holiness, sanctification, is **a divine encounter**. A call to holiness is a call to encounter the living God. My husband was a classical violinist who studied music all his life. Yet, when the call came from God to follow Him, ten years of undergraduate and graduate work at three conservatories was set aside for the ministry.

When God brought Israel out of Egypt and gave them His spiritual and social laws of behavior, His purpose was not to burden their lives with endless rules to keep. He was dividing Israel from the order of the world to bring about total separation of His people from the heathen practices they were already indulging in with increasing frequency. God was not only separating His people from the world, He was preparing them for a divine encounter with Himself.

God is doing this again today, not by the Law but by His Holy Spirit. He is calling His people to separate themselves, to "*be not conformed to the world*" (Rom. 12:2 KJV), but to be transformed by His Spirit that they might be holy. . . prepared for a divine encounter. . . as well as helping others to experience their own divine encounter.

Those of you who read my first book on revival, "*The Fresh Anointing*," will recall the story of Donna, the vivacious young wife and mother whose engineer husband lost his job during the Northeast money crunch. Being unskilled, Donna took what work she could find, which ultimately led her to nursing care for the elderly. Over the past three years, Donna has led more than 150 people to the Lord before they departed this world.

I had a chat with Donna recently and gleaned another outstanding miracle of revival's glorious work in her life. It all began when Pastor Paul received a call to visit a relatively young woman who had only a short time to live. We went immediately to the hospital where this mother in her late forties was being kept in intensive care. Finding her fully awake and aware, Pastor Paul came straight to the point of eternity. Amazingly, the woman said casually,

"No, I do not want to receive Jesus today. I'm having company this afternoon and tomorrow, and I just don't want to think about that right now." Although she was pleasant, the woman talked as though she had just been offered an evening out when she really needed to stay home and get ready for dinner guests.

"Do you mind if we pray for you?" Paul inquired.

"No, it's okay to pray if you want to." She said, seemingly detached from the situation. We prayed and left. Later that week, the woman's family called again. As believers they were desperate, for no one seemed to be able to get through to her.

As her condition deteriorated, the dying women was placed in Donna's unit at the hospital. Donna was notified by the family and she began immediately to establish a friendship with the woman. Time was running out, yet Donna did not feel she should press the woman for a commitment. While on duty a few days later, Donna felt God was saying, *"Go now and speak to a certain elderly patient (who was in the room with the dying woman) and I will save both of them."*

Being careful not to arouse the suspicion of the other nurses, Donna waited for an opening. When it came, she went quietly to the elderly patient God had directed her to, and she found this patient totally open to receive Jesus. Two hours later, the elderly woman passed into eternity. Donna then went to the woman who had been so resistant to us and her family. Drawing from some of her own hurts in life, Donna began her last appeal. This time the woman responded and began to open up and talk about her own life. In a natural sequence of events, Donna came to the question of Jesus. "Yes, I would like to receive Jesus," the woman said, and they prayed together.

Pastor Paul had opportunity to make two further visits to intensive care after this event. "She is confident that she is at peace with God," he said. Two weeks from the time Donna and the woman prayed, she passed peacefully into eternity. Donna's is a good work for which God has sanctified her. She loves her patients and they love and lean on her support. Donna has been sanctified by her loving heavenly Father, fashioned into a divinely empowered and placed messenger at the portal between life and death.

An Encounter with the Truth About Death

Since revival has come, God has repeatedly reminded me that the Church must change its fatalistic vocabulary regarding those who die in the Lord. "She is fighting for her life," one friend said of the lady she cares for. "And I know she loves the Lord."

"Tell her she will never lose her life, only her body for a temporary season," the Spirit immediately prompted me to respond. Death of the body faces every human being. It can be both threatening and painful, but we do not have to bow down to fear's dread and mourn as those who have no destiny in God.

The Church has been robbed far too long concerning the experience of death. For centuries we have mourned as those who have no hope, when the Church is actually the only people who have this hope: Believers have a different destiny than the unbelievers! *The Lord himself shall descend from heaven with a shout. . .and the dead in Christ shall rise. . ."* (1 Thess. 4:16 KJV). Knowing God makes a difference in death, in all kinds of deaths, both of people and situations. We need an encounter with this vital truth again so we will strip off all the trappings of a fearful world. Revival has come to help us take off our grave clothes.

An Encounter with Forgiveness

Every pastor's nightmare is the spiritual death called a "church split." Church division is a very serious thing. *"He that soweth discord among the brethren"* is one of the seven things God hates most (Prov. 6:19 KJV).

After surviving the initial planting of our church in a major American city, our small beginnings began to expand. Eventually we bought our own building and moved in with great anticipation. New church building, more space—we believed it was inevitable that we were bound to grow. This is what the experts on church growth had told us. How foolish of us all to believe we can orchestrate God's works. Buildings do not build churches. *"Except the Lord build the house, they labour in vain that build it. . . ,"* (Ps. 127:1 KJV) the Psalmist warned.

On the heels of our disappointment, born out of the misconception that physical moves can bring real growth to spiritual houses, we soon began to encounter a barrage of murmurings and complaining from the staff. The new facility had not done for them what they had anticipated. By the second year at our new address, a key ministry in the church (which involved forty of our members) went awry. Fast on the heels of this shaking, we and our youth pastor with his extended family parted company under very adverse circumstances.

Needless to say, all kinds of reports began circulating about Christian Teaching and Worship Center. "It must be financial indiscretion," some said. "Judgment has fallen on their hidden character," said others.

Bewildered and battling every natural urge to quit, grace alone kept our hands to the plow. Instead of the growth we had hoped for, we found our numbers rapidly diminishing. Although the Spirit was present and we were known for our teaching, there was a growing slumber over the congregation. This is when we finally surrendered and said, "Lord, if you don't move, what can we do? What can mortal man do that the mighty God has not first initiated?"

In November 1993, after encountering the fresh anointing at a pastor's conference in Georgia with our friends Bill and Dorothy Jean Ligon, revival was birthed within our own congregation. The slumber evaporated. Shortly thereafter, I began to receive invitations to share our new experiences. Two years had gone by since our painful church divisions, and now things were suddenly looking better. At one of these invitations for a local Aglow chapter, I stood to speak. To my utter shock, as I looked back in the audience, I realized that the chapter advisor was our former youth pastor whom I had not seen since our bitter parting. As soon as a glorious anointing was coming to a close in that meeting, I rushed back without hesitation and embraced this pastor with all my heart. He, in turn, embraced me. We cried, we laughed, we blamed ourselves. It was literally as if all our hurts and wounds melted and ran down onto the floor in a moment of time.

Phones began to ring the next day. Apologies and forgiveness began to flow like honey from heaven. There was no rehashing, no recriminations, no counseling necessary. When people work closely together, both inflict wounds against their God-arranged relationship. But when the Spirit presides, the wounds of the flesh will be kept in perspective and love will *"cover a multitude of sins"* (Jas. 5:20 NKJV).

What can I say to glorify God as He deserves in this great spiritual awakening that is taking place today? His power is restoring wounded relationships that were impossible to set right through human counsel. The truth is, we trained our youth pastor and his wife for five years and we loved them and their extended family. They loved us as well, but attitudes developed, both deservedly and undeservedly, and we parted ways. In the world, this might work. In the family of God it is a grief to the Father, and He will go to any extent to rectify the matter.

Today our former youth minister, his wife and family are back with us. We are *"forgetting those things which are behind"* so that we may all *"press toward the mark of the prize of the high calling of God"* that He has set before us (Phil. 3:13,14 KJV). We now have a relationship and a friendship that is twice sweet.

A definite highlight of this revival is "forgiveness," for restoration is rooted in forgiveness. Forgiveness is a great elixir in God's medicine chest. If we could have done everything without making any mistakes, Jesus would not have had to die. For the sake of Christ's great sacrifice of love alone, we are bound to forgive others. His death is a continual reminder that forgiveness is the cure. Even if we could go back and attach blame in all the appropriate places—even if every person involved says they were sorry—there will still be the need to forgive and go on if genuine healing is to occur.

A young Hispanic mother came to me during one meeting, with tears swimming in her eyes. "Six years ago I had terrible depression. I cried out to God and in a minute's time—it was gone. Please help me understand what is taking place now. My sixteen-year-old son is under psychiatric care and taking medication for anxiety. I, too, am having to fight it. It's the history of my family back in my country. But I see joy flowing in the church and I want it for my son and me."

She and thousands of others have "thought" themselves into emotional misery. Recognizing this, I began to exhort her by saying, "You encourage your own troubles by the way you think—the things you give your attention to. The more depressed or anxious you are, the more you examine your thoughts, your past and your circumstances. Stop examining yourselves and begin to examine God. Spend your thought time pressing into Him, understanding Him, thinking about the way He is. As you understand more about God, you will understand more about yourself. Search yourself and you will just find confusion and missing pieces. Search God and more understanding of His ways, and you will find the missing pieces of your own life."

I have learned this truth from personal experience. I have never found peace by searching my own life and thoughts. Only as I stop digging into my own empty wells and admit that I can never fill in all the missing pieces, do I really allow God to be God.

Then I said to this mother who was battling a history of family depression, "I can't promise that Satan will not be back. Jesus made it clear that he continually peeks into all our lives to see if there is room for him (see Matt. 12:45). But I can promise that if your thoughts are occupied with God, nothing will be able to unseat God. I encourage you to get into the stream of the joy you now see flowing in the church and you will drown your depression!"

Discord and mental oppression are two strongholds we see God challenging head on with this revival. Improved attitudes are among the most frequent healings, and a great majority of the victories are won as people abandon themselves to worship and celebration of God. The attitude of our entire church has been radically altered through the presence of divine joy and shouting during worship.

Revival is calling us to come apart from the "plagues" of this present age and to get on with the business of the kingdom. But the first business of priority for each of us is our own personal "divine encounter. Spirit-controlled worship, more than any one single thing we can do, will bring about that life-changing encounter. When anyone comes to us today seeking change, we place worship at the top of the list. It is God's lifelong medication for healing our ills.

I like to think that I am a "well-balanced" person when it comes to acknowledging the realities of this present world. I am not given to tangents or spiritual histrionics. Both Paul and I are cautious in every decision we make, from buying an appliance for our home to introducing new methods in the church. But the day we allowed the Holy Spirit to release worship in our church was the greatest decision of our ministry. Not only are we encountering God for ourselves, but every person who comes into our services hungry for an encounter finds Him!

There are numerous areas of encounters with God throughout a lifetime, but none as important as worship. Worship brings us into His presence. It sets us apart from all other people.

7

The Sanctifying Work of Revival

"But know that the Lord hath set apart him that is godly for himself . . ." (Ps. 4:3 KJV).

To the vast majority, this present world is seen as the only viable offer. This is due in part to the Church's illusion about maintaining a "private faith" that has confined its total experience with God to one hour of religious expression on Sunday morning. Timed, rehearsed and polished for hundreds of years, Christian worship services have now been conveniently reduced to a wafer and sip of wine, a processional, two hymns, the offering, a homily, the recessional and the dinner bell greets the opening of the doors. We could set our watches by our church doors. Closed at eleven—service begins; open at twelve—service ends.

It is no wonder that revival—with its erratic, disruptive pattern—is having difficulty being received by the "well-formed" Church. The phrase "quiet as a church mouse" should tell the Church something about its reputation since philosophic intellectualism revamped the Day of Pentecost. To be sure, our form, our structure, our ability to move with the clock is whistle clean. But how spiritually formed, how spiritually attuned is the Church to the will of the Holy Spirit?

Paul said, *"This is the will of God, even your sanctification"* (1 Thess. 4:3 KJV). In the Old Testament, "things" (which cannot sin) were sanctified. All the vessels in the tabernacle were anointed and sanctified for God's use. Specific men were anointed and set apart to handle those vessels. Those men were priests sanctified for sacred purpose.

Sanctification in its broadest sense is to separate ones life from the influence of fallen nature to the control of the Holy Spirit. A truly spiritual person is one whose whole life is a praise to God. Whether at work, at play, at rest, when eating, or worshipping, or going about the business of the day, a spiritual person is doing all things to the glory of God. This makes the farmer, the banker and the evangelist on equal footing in God's eyes. Plato's dicotic view of man was incorrect. This natural world is not evil. Everything God created was good. Plato called man's body a grave but God called it a temple. Anything this temple does by the leading of the Holy Spirit is good works and will reap eternal reward. Revival comes to call men back to their priestly roles—personally as well as for specific assignments.

Separating Flesh from Pride

A Greek orthodox cantor and his wife began attending the Monday evening services of our church. When revival broke out, the wife entered in and began to flow in the Holy Spirit's leadings. Her ever-proper, fifty-five-year-old husband said with some annoyance, "Get control of yourself!"

His wife responded, "But the Holy Spirit is moving me to laugh and lie on the floor before Him."

"Then how come He doesn't tell me to do such things, too? You can control yourself—I do!" the husband retorted.

The services continued for several months and gradually the cantor entered more and more into the flow of the service. At first he began to sing the Psalms in Greek and translate them into English. He then took another step and began to dance before the Lord. Finally, on one Sunday morning (more than eight months into the revival), this traditionally reserved worshiper began to leap and sing during worship. Then he suddenly hit the floor, turned a somersault and leaped to his feet laughing, looking every bit as stunned as those of us who were watching.

"I couldn't do that on my own if you begged me to," he said later. "But I just felt God asking me to allow the Holy Spirit to separate my flesh from pride, and I obeyed. After I did it [the somersault], God spoke to my heart and said, 'This is my house. Tell my children their Father invites them to enjoy themselves.'" Enjoying God. What a concept!

Enjoying our God is a far more spiritual act than many of our so-called great works. There is no higher spiritual work than giving glory to God, and worship is the primary setting for this work. Holy Spirit-led worship is sanctification in action. Public worship is sanctification made visible.

Christianity is very personal, but it is not and was never intended to be purely private. Why would God set people apart, call them to public assembly and commission them to make His name known everywhere if all He wanted was a "private" faith practiced in seclusion? The work of the Holy Spirit is both private and public. He works privately within each believer to produce an outworking of spiritual grace and witness to others.

A new song to come out of the present revival says, "I am changed, changed, changed, I will never be the same." Tomorrow, I will not be what I am today. Next month, I will not be what I am tomorrow. Anyone flowing with the ongoing program of the living God will live in a state of continual change bringing about separation from the world and its ways. It is this "change" that works its way through our lives and into the public arena.

A young woman came to our Church one evening. "I have driven by here for the past four weeks," she confessed. "I knew if I stopped, I would be forever changed. I also knew I would never again enjoy a church that is not spiritually alive." Life cannot remain static. When any living thing ceases to change and develop, death begins to take over. Jesus said, *"I am come that you might have life and that more abundantly"* (John 10:10 paraphrased). Jesus' coming to earth has put this world into a state of spiritual change.

Superficial Treasures

For the past 2,000 years, we have been encountering repeated spiritual explosions. Principalities and powers are waging their last efforts at world control as they see the program of God advancing toward the Millennium. We as the Church are caught up in this electrifying change. Publicly, we are a threat. The world senses the ongoing momentum of a Church alive with the Spirit of God, and it knows instinctively that its system's days are numbered.

The world system is running dry. The world desperately needs change, recharging, something to "pump it up." That is why it has literally scraped the bottom of the barrel to search out new levels of shocking anti-God filth, looking for a new thrill. The apparent motive seems to be that any jolt of recharging is better than nothing. Yet, God is drawing a people right out of the midst of this morass. A stranger came down to the altar one evening, saying, "Last week you told my wife that you saw her husband with a wine bottle to his mouth trying to squeeze out the last drop. I am that thirsty, spiritually dry person. I want to be changed. I want to be filled and refreshed by God's Spirit!"

The Holy Spirit is God the Spirit. This makes His presence within each of us a sobering reality. If you are a believer, you have a divine presence within you at all times and in every situation you will ever face. This divine guest is not only resident within you, He is actively working in your life according to God's desires.

Desire

Desire is a major force in human nature. It drives men to all kinds of extremes. There seems to be no limits as to what a person will do out of strong desire for good or for evil. For this reason, one of the functions of the Holy Spirit is to confront every desire that sets itself against God. From the moment you were filled with the Spirit, He set His desire against your flesh. "*. . . Walk by the Spirit, and you will not carry out the desire of the flesh. For the flesh sets its desire against the Spirit, and the Spirit against the flesh. . .*" (Gal. 5:16,17 NAS).

The flesh and the Spirit are in absolute opposition to each other as the sanctifying process gets under way. The Apostle Paul explains that we who are led by the desires of the flesh cannot please God, "*. . .For if ye live after the flesh, ye shall die*" (Rom. 8:13 KJV). It is the Holy Spirit's duty to see that you and I become separated from the ways of death, the ways of the flesh, to produce spiritual works unto God. This is not a work of the human will, this is a work of the Spirit. As we consciously choose to obey the Holy Spirit, He empowers us to resist the sins of the flesh and to do the works of the Spirit.

What are the personal results of the sanctified life? We develop in character. *"Love, joy, peace, longsuffering, gentleness, goodness, faith, meekness, temperance* [self-control]. . ." become a way of life (Gal. 5:22,23 KJV). The characteristics, or qualities, that make us decent and enjoyable human beings overtake our tendencies to be selfish and cruel. One of the key works of this present revival is the renewing of the inner personality, a restoration of Christ-like characteristics. I have observed dozens of people being gradually put back together as whole human beings.

A young girl, with two children born out of wedlock, came to our church years ago from a nearby housing project. After years of parental abuse and incest, the girl received and accepted an offer of marriage. Pastor Paul was asked to perform the ceremony in his office. I watched her walk away on the day of her wedding looking more like a wilted flower than a young girl beginning a fresh dream. From that day forward I do not recall ever seeing a real smile on this young woman's face. Although her marriage remained intact, everything about her just seemed to droop—until the revival. On the first day of revival, when I so longed to see everyone rejoicing, this same young woman was so full of sadness her tears felt hot as they splashed on my hands when I prayed with her. As she turned to walk back to her chair, I felt as angry as she felt discouraged. For once in her life, I wanted desperately to see a smile on her face.

One year has passed since that day, and what has revival done for this sorrowful bride? She is laughing, dancing, clapping her hands and celebrating. She is being set apart from all her sorrows to serve the Lord. Together with her husband, these two are being sanctified from everything that once pulled them down, and they are leading people to the Lord on a regular basis. Their home is becoming a house of witness to other broken lives looking for real peace and joy.

The Social Results

Society is changed by individuals who have been changed. Every selfish and destructive trait we hate in ourselves and in others can be changed when the Holy Spirit is free to challenge our wrong desires. Every good trait we long to experience in ourselves and others can be achieved when the Holy Spirit is free to express His abilities through us.

I once watched a Jewish Rabbi, as he was lecturing on the subject of today's society, respond to the question of how we could change society. His answer was very wise: "There is no society that enables the individual. Society is a myth. It is made up of individuals. If you want to change society, change an individual."

"Society" has neither the power to enable nor disable individuals. The choices we make and the actions we take in response to our society and to our God are what determines our futures. The "myth" that society can either empower individuals to succeed or be the cause of their failures is what has brought America to the state she is now in. All of man's Band-Aid remedies for the ills of society are coming loose, and we are finally realizing that we are inadequate to make any substantial changes in the real world. What we need is a worldwide revival of repentance and turning again to God.

Revivals are times of refreshing. Just as houses and apartments need a face-lift now and then, God's temples need periodic refurbishing in a spiritual sense. According to Webster's Dictionary, the word "refresh" means to reinvigorate and stimulate. Christians certainly need to be reinvigorated and stimulated—emotionally, mentally and spiritually—from time to time. We need a fresh spiritual zeal to wash in upon our tendency to stagnate.

Times of Refreshing

"Repent therefore and be converted, that your sins may be blotted out, so that times of refreshing may come from the presence of the Lord" (Acts 3:19 NKJV).

This "refreshing" literally means to "recover your breath." As we come to the end of this century, the Church has run out of breath—but the race is not yet over! God has brought His presence into our midst to revive us with times of refreshing. He has some great battles ahead for us to win!   A brand new millennium is upon us. Restoration—not annihilation—is coming. Our houses are built on the Rock and, recovering our breath, we are called to stand firm in a system that is failing all around us.

It has been our experience in the local church here in Boston, as well as in other nations, that the Spirit is washing in upon the Church with refreshing waves of invigorating power. We are getting our "second wind" and picking up momentum once again. Reports of victory and change are literally piling up in our office faster than we can tabulate them. People who have just "occupied seats" in the sanctuary for years are coming alive. Our church is literally getting new legs.

I noticed an elderly woman in deep worship during a service. As we were nearing the close, she came forward saying, "I've got to share what God has done! My legs have been in such pain I could hardly walk. Tonight God has touched my legs! I can even run!" And off she went—running with new vigor. Several months have gone by and she is still worshipping with the same vitality.

One strong, athletic couple in our church got a vision for youth several years ago. They founded "Christian Youth Athletics" for New England, reaching out to approximately 1,000 children in the metropolitan Boston area year round. So effective was their work, the mayor of the city of Woburn officially declared a "Steve and Diane Arsenault Day." On a Sunday morning, we announced this honor to the church, read the plaque and congratulated Steve and Diane. The morning service concluded and with much well wishing and congratulations, we all went our separate ways.

That afternoon Steve took a nap at his home. When he woke up, the right side of his face was paralyzed, his eye would not close and his mouth hung open. We were called for prayer. The next day Steve was diagnosed as having Bell's Palsy. "You should not expect to recover from this for at least three months. Full or partial recovery may be expected," the doctor said.

Steve came by the church that week for prayer, and the next day word came that his face looked worse. "But we're trusting God in spite of the way things look," Diane said. Two weeks later on Sunday, Steve came to church. A thunderous applause went up to God when Steve came down. His face was totally restored and far ahead of schedule!

There have been many physical, emotional and spiritual changes in the people who have entered into the revival.

Young men with stringy hair and dangling earrings are coming forward saying, "I want my life changed." Young men embarking on promising careers are lifting their hands before the Lord and singing about change. Older men and women are coming into the services and reaching out for a fresh touch from God. We see the Spirit calling people of every stature of life to separate themselves and enter into the Spirit-controlled life, sanctified for His purposes. According to the following Scriptures, the sanctified person is one who:

1) Knows God the Father (Jude 1).
2) Has come to the Father through Christ Jesus (1 Cor. 1:2, 6:11; Heb. 10:10,29).
3) Has been "born again" by the Spirit (John 3:16).
4) Is continually filled with (comes under the control of) the Holy Spirit (Rom. 15:16; 1 Pet. 1:2).
5) Lives according to the Word of God (Eph. 5:26).
6) Has active faith in God (Acts 26:18).
7) Measures truth by God's Word (John 17:9).

This is very aptly summed up in a quote from Azusa Street:

"We continue to have wonderful meetings at Eighth and Maple. The Lord showed me he wanted this work to go deeper yet than anything we had at that time attained to.... There was still too much of the self-life, the religious self, among us. This naturally meant war, hard and bitter, from the enemy. Ours was to be a sort of 'clearing station' where fleshly exercises, false manifestations, and the religious self in general should be dealt with. We were after real experiences, permanent and established, with God-like character, and no relapses." (*Azusa Street*, Frank Bartleman, Bridge Publishing, pg. 79)

"Real experiences, permanent and established, with God-like character and no relapses." This, I believe, describes a sanctified person very well. This is also what I see God working to accomplish in His Church in this revival. God has a work for sanctified people. He wants to raise them up to be princes of His glory, as the next chapter explains.

8

Set Among Princes

Thirty-five-hundred years ago, a woman prophesied some amazing things about God and the way He moves among men on the earth. One enlightening revelation Hannah spoke is very meaningful to us in this day of revival. Samuel records Hannah's words concerning God:

> *"He raiseth up the poor out of the dust, and lifteth up the beggar from the dunghill, to set them among princes, and to make them inherit the throne of glory: for the pillars of the earth are the Lord's, and he hath set the world upon them"* (1 Sam. 2:8 KJV).

In other words, God laid the foundations of the earth, He is Creator and rightful owner of all things, and He is rightfully able to lift up the humble and set them in high places. The Church certainly needs lifting up today. Physically afflicted, emotionally wounded, spiritually weakened, the Church is in need of a touch from God. The Psalmist said the fact that God does lift up His people from the dust is reason to praise Him:

> *"Praise Ye the Lord. Praise, O ye servants of the Lord, praise the name of the Lord. Blessed be the name of the Lord from this time forth and for evermore. From the rising of the sun unto the going down of the same the Lord's name is to be*

> *praised. . . .He raiseth up the poor out of the dust, and lifteth the needy out of the dunghill; that he may set him with princes, even with the princes of his people"* (Ps.113:1-3, 7-8 KJV).

What a blessed people we are who know the Lord! What honor is accorded us, the Church, by the Lord. To know that He has promised He will raise us from the dust and set us among princes! We will not be set among the princes of this world whose thrones are being toppled daily, but we are being set among God's princes who sit *"together in the heavenly places in Christ Jesus"* (Eph. 2:6 NKJV). We are set among people invested with God's power and commission.

The Dunghill

According to the Word of God, the destiny of this world system, and all who are a part of it, is the dunghill or the rubbish heap. To be sentenced to the dunghill is a judgment from ancient times. Daniel 2:5 records Nebuchadnezzar threatening the Chaldeans with the dunghill unless they interpreted his dream; *". . . Ye shall be cut in pieces, and your houses shall be made a dunghill"* (KJV).

Interestingly enough, this decree of Nebuchadnezzar was also stated by Ezra some years later as a threat to God's people. After Ezra had given the word of the Lord to the people, listen to what he said:

> *"Also, I have made a decree, that whosoever shall alter this word, let timber be pulled down from his house, and being set up, let him be hanged thereon; and let his house be made a dunghill for this"* (Ezra 6:11 KJV).

But the threat of the dunghill was not simply confined to the people of ancient times. In speaking of all believers, Jesus said:

*"Salt is good: but if the salt have lost his savor [saltiness].
. . . It is neither fit for the land, nor yet for the dunghill; but
men cast it out. He that hath ears to hear, let him hear"* (Luke
14:34,35 KJV).

God sends His revivals to us because the cares of this
world can become so big and important to us, we lose our
spiritual saltiness. We may look like salt and we may
shake like salt, but when we are sprinkled on a situation,
we fall flat! Without divine saltiness, we have no power or
spiritual effectiveness to bring out the divine flavor in
situations. We go into the world, act like the world, whine
and complain like the world, and reduce ourselves to the
world's methods for solving our problems.

A friend called me recently and said, "We just had a
minister with a great anointing at our church. But he left a
bitter taste in our mouth. On the last night of the meetings,
because he had received only a $27,000 offering from our
congregation, he spent one hour pushing until he received a
total of $40,000 for one of his upcoming crusades. What
do you think of that?" she questioned.

"I think it is serious carnality at work in a man of God.
And it's one reason God is sending revival fires. He is
going to cleanse the Church of man's manipulative
methods that operate under the guise of ministry."
Spiritually empowered people do not have to beg or
manipulate and, in so doing, shame the Gospel. Many
good ministers need to learn this fact—and lay down their
carnal methods.

According to Jesus, carnal saltlessness does not even
qualify for the dunghill. But just exactly what is a dunghill,
since it gets several mentions in the Scriptures? One of the
gates in Jerusalem is even named the Dung Gate, the place
where all manure and refuse was discarded from within the
city.

Manure or dung in Hebrew is *zebel*—from which we get Zibbul, which means idolatrous sacrifice. It is also where we get one of Satan's titles—Beelzebub. The world may well be consumed with its idols, but the Church has no excuse for such sin. Idol worship is a major force on the earth today, and Satan is lord of all idol worship which is equal to manure in God's sight. Not only do we all admire, and even idolize, pagan objects, idolizing human achievements and human achievers has also become our passion.

Idol Worship

On one of our trips abroad Paul and I were invited into a Christian minister's office where we were shocked to find that he had a collection of Communist art—busts of Lenin, paintings of Stalin, Nazi helmets. "What are you doing?" we asked him.

We were shocked to hear his proud reply, "This is history," he replied. "I am going to sell it to museums in the United States and use the money to spread the Gospel."

Communism is a demonic power on the earth which is still alive. It is only being held in abeyance by God so revival can flourish in parts of the world where the satanic principality of communism has ruled. To create and preserve busts of Lenin and paintings of Stalin is to humanize demonic powers and help to deceive the next generation. To see Stalin with a twinkle in his eyes, friendly, laughing, is to put a human face on a demonic murder machine.

Symbols of communism or any other evil power are not art that deserve to be preserved. They are manure and deserve to be thrown out on the dunghill. Our youngest son saw some of the boys in his high school wearing communist military garb shortly after the fall of the Iron Curtain. "I want one of those coats," our son remarked.

After careful consideration, we said to Joshua, "This military garb once represented fear, intimidation and death to millions. Do you really want to wear this kind of symbol?" He wisely responded that he did not.

The Holy Spirit is bringing revival to the Church today because we need to have our affections purged from compromise with the idols of this world. Abraham avinu taught us clearly that people of the true faith are *"sojourners"* and *"tent dwellers"* (see Heb. 11). We are people who are called out of idol worship to know the living God who allows no other gods.

For 6,000 years God has been giving man glimpses of Himself. When men's eyes become heavy and too many idols get between God and His creation, God moves in ways that jar people awake and cause their idols to fall.

The Cross

Since the Holy Spirit was poured out on our congregation in 1993, our eyes have been opened to many practices and beliefs we took for granted. At the front of our sanctuary we have a menorah on one side and a cross on the other. I started through the sanctuary recently, when suddenly a stream of thoughts hit me: The menorah was a pattern given by God when Moses was instructed to make a candlestick patterned after the candlestick in heaven's temple (see Exod. 25:31-40), but the cross was originally a heathen sign designed by man. The symbol of the cross is found in most pagan cultures of the Middle East from Egypt to Assyria. The menorah represents life. The cross represents death. Rome used the cross as a means of execution.

"But Jesus died on a cross," I responded to these thoughts.

And the Spirit responded to me, *"Yes, but the cross did not save man. The shed blood of Jesus atoned for man's sin. Millions of Christians respect the cross, but they have no idea what the life and blood of Jesus mean. The cross has been designed into a piece of jewelry that unbelievers as well as believers wear. The cross makes people feel religious when, in fact, they may not be at all. But the shed blood of Jesus has no beauty for anyone except the truly repentant."*

God warns His people about the power of images. One of Israel's greatest snares throughout their long history was the turning of memorials into shrines of worship. When Gideon led Israel to victory, he would take no glory or position for himself when it was offered. Instead he built a memorial as a reminder of God's deliverance. But instead of remembering God, the people began to worship the shrine. It became a snare to them, robbing them of a clear focus of God.

The symbol of the cross is not wrong. Scripture tells us that Jesus *"endured the cross, despising the shame"* (Heb. 12:2 KJV). Jesus died for the sins of the world on a cross. He also used the cross as a symbol of death to the carnal life, saying, *"Whoever does not bear his cross and come after Me cannot be My disciple"* (Luke 14:27 NKJV). In at least ten references, Paul used the cross to signify the plan of redemption. But, overemphasis on any one thing occludes other important aspects of the truth.

The cross was made by man. It can be, and is, duplicated by the pagan world. On the other hand, no man can duplicate the soul-cleansing blood of Jesus—its value is beyond anything made by man. The cross was the vehicle, but His blood gave the life. The cross was not even a symbol in the Church until the third century A.D., but the blood was there from the moment of Jesus' ascension. Our focus must not be the cross, but the One who died on the cross. Revival is identifying Christ once again for a generation gone severely out of focus.

Saved

Another truth God recently restored to me is the term "saved." Jesus told Nicodemus, *"Most assuredly, I say to you, unless one is born again, he cannot see the kingdom of God"* (John 3:3 NKJV). It is scriptural to use the term "born again." However, in numerous passages of Scripture, "saved" and "lost" are used to describe the two sides of man's spiritual condition. I think that is very helpful, for I may have some difficulty understanding a new birth, a second birth, but I know what it means to be lost. Lost people need to be found; lost things need to be sought after. And Jesus said He came *"to seek and to save that which was lost"* (Luke 19:10 NKJV).

Entertainers, politicians, psychologists, and other professionals have picked up this spiritual term and seem to love to talk about being "born again" when they find a new career opportunity, fresh inspiration or even a divorce. They also talk about "finding" themselves. How can a lost person "find himself?" If you are lost in the woods, finding yourself won't get you out of your dilemma. What a lost person needs is not to find himself, but he needs to find a "way out" for himself. Jesus said there was only one "way" out: *"I am the way, the truth, and the life"* (John 14:6 NKJV).

Along with the terms "saved" and "born again," the Church needs to restore the vivid picture of a soul that is "lost." If one does not really understand the immense tragedy of being lost, how can one understand the exhilaration of being found? When the Church renews this understanding, then God's people will also understand the joy and the laughter of those whose souls have been "found" and rescued by God.

A young northwestern couple and their baby were lost for eight days in a terrible blizzard. Whole teams of people went out in search of them. What joy and laughter covered their faces when they were finally found and taken to safety. What applause went up from the teams who brought them in to a safe haven. Rescued people have genuine cause to celebrate their rescue and their Rescuer!

Roots

Today it has become popular to identify with one's roots. But if we all go back far enough we will find heathen roots in our family tree and the many ills that go with idol worship. This answers for much of the present demonic influence the United States of America is experiencing. Through music, fashion and re-education, our youth have been encouraged to adopt the gods of their ancestors. In the past thirty five years we have made giant leaps backwards toward our idol-cursed heritage. Europe, Asia, Africa, the Americas, Australia and the islands were all originally idol worshipers, barbaric and violent. As the Gospel spread, the principalities and powers of Satan were subdued and the continents developed a measure of human civility.

But in recent years, the tide has washed back upon our natural roots. So many Americans have renounced God and turned back in search of their pagan heritage. Without a second thought, we wear the jewelry, adopt the fashions and hair styles, delve into the occult history and promote the immoral behavior common to idol worshipers. Through romanticizing our forefather's cultures, we have become ensnared and returned to their curse of violence.

Is our cultural heritage evil? Some of it is and needs to be forgotten forever. Other parts of our heritage are not necessarily evil unless they are allowed to supersede God's will for the Christian family. When culture hinders people from worshipping and working together for the kingdom of heaven's sake, it is evil. When a culture isolates people and makes them suspicious of everyone outside its traditions, it is evil. When culture causes us to personally live in contradiction to the Word of God, it is evil. Anything that competes with God, His Word or His work is evil. From the outset we have been warned by God Himself in the Ten Commandments, *"You shall have no other gods before Me"* (Deut. 5:7 NKJV).

Since revival has come, God has been pulling down our idols. One night, while I was alone in a hotel room, God began to shine His light upon "my idols." I was shocked at what I discovered. Taking a pen I began to write down my prayer:

> *"Heavenly Father, I ask you to purge from my heart every pedestal on which I have exalted myself—seeking to share in the glory that belongs only to God.*

> *"Purge me from seeking 'eternal youth' for a body that is justly condemned to pass away."*
> (As I prayed these words, God showed me the spirit behind the world's obsession with youth. We are a generation seeking to deny death of the flesh in its present cursed state. We want to achieve eternal existence without God.)

> *"Purge me from seeking the same beauty the world seeks."*
> (The world is obsessed with appearance. Beauty has been redefined as having an appearance of sexiness, power,

liberation. It is an appearance the Church has bought into, supposedly for the purpose of "reaching out" to all people. First Thessalonians 5:22 says to "abstain from all appearance of evil," and to reach out with the good news of the Gospel.)

"Purge me from seeking the same longevity the world seeks."
(The world is jogging and "working out" in hopes of acquiring eternal mortality, in place of the "transforming immortality" given only by God. While I believe in reasonable physical exercise, I temper time given to it with Paul's wisdom, "For bodily exercise profits little, but godliness profits in all things, both in this life and in the world to come" 1 Tim 4:8.)

"Purge me from seeking the same fame the world seeks."
(God dealt with me about seeking to have my name known as a minister. Fame-seeking for a believer is glory seeking, and God shares His glory with no one. Fame is not wrong when awarded to a person, and God does use fame for His purposes. Famous godly men and women are an inspiration. But fame and fame-seeking are of two different spirits.)

"Purge me from all desire to merchandise the Gospel for the sake of making anyone other than Christ known."
(I believe revival is going to reduce the amount of big, shiny promotional brochures God's people think they need. When God's power is sufficiently present, any necessary information can be conveyed in a few words.)

"Lord, close my eyes to that which would impress my carnal heart, and open the pupils of my spirit that I may discern Your voice today. Purge from my heart every pedestal on which I have exalted anything that competes for the glory that belongs only to God."

This was the prayer I wrote down that day and one I continue to pray over my life.   The glory of man is fading fast. One day it will all return to the dust. God wants to lift His people out of the dirt and set us among princes who know how to live in divine authority and holy character now.

The Call to See

One main facet of this present revival is the call to lift our vision above the pathetic blindness of this hour. The lack of sound thinking today is phenomenal. As of May 27, 1994, the New English-Language Catechism of the Catholic Church reads: "The plan of salvation also includes those who acknowledge the Creator, in the first place amongst whom are the Muslims."

Many among the Protestants would also agree with this unholy position, adopting the position of awarding salvation to the Muslims. The Muslim's "bible," the Qur'an (or Koran: The book of religious writing purported to be revelation given to Muhammad by Allah through the angel Gabriel) rejects the Bible as it is written. In fact, the Qur'an has totally altered biblical salvation truths. To quote only a fraction of the contradictions between the Qur'an and the Bible:

The Qur'an rejects the divinity of Jesus, saying: "Christ the son of Mary was no more than an apostle. . . ." (Sura 5:73-75).

> *"In the beginning was the Word, and the Word was with God, and the Word was God. . . . And the Word was made flesh, and dwelt among us, and we beheld his glory, the glory as of the only begotten of the Father, full of grace and truth"* (John 1:1,14 KJV).

The Qur'an denies Christ's Sonship: "Allah, the eternal, absolute He begetteth not, nor is he begotten . . ." (Sura 112:2,3)

> *"For God so loved the world, that he gave his only begotten Son, that whosoever believes in him should not perish, but have everlasting life"* (John 3:16 KJV).

The Qur'an denies Jesus' death and atoning work on which the Christian faith rests: ". . . They killed him not, nor crucified him, but so it was made to appear to them," (Sura 4:157)

> *"Then he [Jesus] took the twelve aside and said to them, 'Behold, we are going up to Jerusalem, and all things that are written by the prophets concerning the Son of man will be accomplished. For He will be delivered to the Gentiles and will be mocked and insulted and spit upon. They will scourge Him and kill Him. And the third day He will rise again"* (Luke 18:31-33 NKJV).

How can men award salvation to anyone who denies the Savior and the resurrection? The Church at large has lost the pinions of its faith. We have accommodated the gods of this age until we have lost sight of the truth. This is why societies all over the world are being brought down into the dust. Tribal wars, ethnic cleansings, famine, disease—the whole earth is reeling under the curse of other gods. The United Nations has voted for a global military force, as though numbers and unity of effort will save the human race. But chariots of gold driven by generals of genius will not be able to withstand the coming judgment of God on the worldwide industry of idolatry.

My friend D.J. Ligon was bumping along an exhausting road in one poverty-stricken nation given to idol worship, observing the people literally living in the dirt. God spoke to her and said, "This is where Satan brings all those who worship him—down into the dirt where the serpent was sentenced to exist."

But God says to those who would believe Him: *"He raiseth up the poor out of the dust, and lifteth up the beggar* from the dunghill, to set them among princes, and *to make them inherit the throne of glory. . ."* (1 Sam. 2:8 KJV).

Glory is the manifested presence of the power of God. Revival has come to the Church today to lift us out of the dirt of this world—its plagues, its diseases, its practices, its sentence of death that we might demonstrate His glory. But in order to be lifted up, we must be willing to lay down our idols. Revival is exposing our idols and as we are laying them down, the curses are being lifted.

At a service one evening, Paul was walking down the aisle when he stopped beside a young man who was visiting for the first time. As Paul began to minister to him, the young man stood and then he began to shake and moan. Finally, when Paul commanded in the name of Jesus, a loud cry went out of the young man and he fell back into his chair totally relaxed. The power of Satan is being broken by revival. The method and drama of deliverance varies, but the results are the same. We don't make a shrine out of methods, we look only to the Deliverer Who lifts the humble from the dust and, if they continue in obedience, sets them among princes of spiritual power and soundness.

9

When God Speaks

Man, with all his "things" that he might employ in the work of God, remains but an instrument or a vessel of supply. God in heaven alone is the source of all spiritual awakenings. When revival fires begin to ignite in various parts of the world, we need to listen—God is speaking!

When an earthquake hit Los Angeles and destroyed several blocks of the pornographic industry, some of the leading ministers said, "The judgment of God!" Oddly enough, those ministers were joined by the secular press who declared, "It's enough to make a person lose interest in sin." On the other hand, another voice from other clergy calmly reassured the Church, "This is not the judgment of God, it is a wake-up call to lay down our differences and enter into greater unity."

Which one is right? Was it judgment or a loving call to unity? According to past moves of God, the answer could well be: Both.

In the eighth century B.C., the northern kingdom of Israel had fallen deeply into sin. Two prophets were raised up by God with two different messages. Hosea, whose name means "the Lord saves," was commanded by God to marry a prostitute, to love her and bear children with her.

On several occasions Hosea was forced to go out into the streets looking for his unfaithful wife, and with tears he would entreat her to return to him. This served as an example of God's love for unfaithful Israel.

On the other hand, during this same time, God also raised up Amos, whose name means "to bear a load." It was Amos' mission to become outraged at the violence Israel had done to social justice and righteousness. Judgment was indeed in the mouth of Amos; just listen to his warning:

"Hear this word that the Lord hath spoken against you, O children of Israel, against the whole family which I brought up from the land of Egypt, saying, You only have I known of all the families of the earth: therefore I will punish you for all your iniquities. Can two walk together, except they be agreed?" (Amos 3:1-3 KJV).

All of mankind has compromised the standards of God. We, the Church, have committed adultery with the psychology of the world and frequently sought the world's companionship more than God's. The Church of today is quick to quench the Spirit of God for fear of man's disapproval, slow to judge sin and eager to label the flame of God as "wild fire." As I observe the opinions concerning the various manifestations of the Spirit in this present revival—especially the laughter—I see the Church often more tolerant of immoral people than laughing people.

Once again, the loving call of Hosea is being sent out to the Church to come out of its compromises and purify itself. The outpourings of joy and laughter are the signs that are drawing the people in. At the same time, the brazen call of Amos is going out to the Church that judgment is coming on all those who condone violence, injustice and unrighteousness. David Wilkerson calls the modern Church the "Eli Ministry." Eli was the priest of Israel who refused to judge the sins of his sons in ministry. Because of his compromise, the whole nation fell and his sons were destroyed.

No one person has the whole scope of God's mind. Let us not be so quick to discredit what comes through the mouth of more than one prophet. Only the counsel of God covers the full picture. Certainly it is within the character of God to judge and act upon a ring of pornography that is poisoning the whole world. At the same time, it is within the nature of His compassion to call for His people to rise up and build bridges of unity and understanding. God is never just judging and destroying, as surely as He is never just building and comforting. How could He, in a world that is continually in need of both purging and building up?

Amos said, *"The lion hath roared; who will not fear? The Lord God hath spoken, who can but prophesy?"* (Amos 3:8 KJV).

Peter quoted the prophet Joel: *"And it shall come to pass in the last days, saith God, I will pour out of my Spirit upon all flesh: and your sons and your daughters shall prophesy, and your young men shall see visions, and your old men shall dream dreams: and on my servants and on my handmaidens I will pour out in those days of my Spirit, and they shall prophesy"* (Acts 2:17-18 KJV).

There will never be a time when God will speak to men on the earth as much as in the last days before Jesus' return.

Multiple words and signs should be expected from within the Church in the days ahead. Words will come not only from the ministers, but God is going to move upon and speak through lay men and women, and they will be unable to restrain themselves from making it known. Young, old, male, female, will speak as oracles of God. There can be no great revivals with just a handful of theologians and fivefold ministers in control—just as there can be no sound revivals without solid theology and wise leadership. There must always be a balance. But it is God who will weigh this revival on the balance scales, and it will not be found wanting!

The Voices of the Twentieth Century

The latter part of the twentieth century will surely record one of the most unusual conscription of voices Church history has ever noted. People of various denominational backgrounds are going to flow in the one stream of Pentecost.

In the last days, God will have men and women of every rank and degree as His spokespeople. The prophecy of the "handmaiden" will be as revelatory as the pronouncements of the great ministers, and the prophecy of the "servant" will be as mighty as the works of the multi-gifted. The anointing of the Lord will bridge the difference. As fires break out spontaneously in parched forests, so will the Spirit of God be poured out upon the thirsty. Great flames shall leap out of the most unlikely places and intense heat will be felt in some of the coldest spots on earth. "Ice" will melt in places thought impossible to evangelize—royal families, Islamic enclaves, ethnic enclaves heretofore closed to the Gospel. Waves of burning intensity will be felt throughout the nations.

The outpourings of the Spirit in these last days will not be silenced, just as it could not be silenced at the first. He will speak in places formerly thought impenetrable even to God's Spirit, refusing to be confined to any one people. When the theologians would silence Peter and John, the formally uneducated, the disciples answered, *"Whether it is right in the sight of God to hearken unto you more than unto God, judge ye. For we cannot but speak the things which we have seen and heard*" (Acts 4:19-20 KJV).

Order, But Not Preference

There is an order of responsibility in God's kingdom, but there is not preference. God does not prefer the man of high ranking responsibility more than any other man or woman, nor does He prefer the low ranking to the high. The call to one is not greater than the call to another. Promotion comes based on obedience to what God has spoken, rather than inherent ability. Obedience is better than the greatest of sacrifices from a disobedient heart.

In 1960, the world took a new direction. Globalism was born in government, in international social networking and in religion. In 1960, nationalism took a fatal blow as it began to be devoured by the "One-World Order" of the one-world army, the one-world political and police government. Nations are now being scrutinized for their every independent action that appears to threaten peace by a concert of United Nations.

In the Western world, all religions have begun to be poured into one big melting pot of New Age humanism. Western man has decided that he will set the religious agenda for the West from now on—not God. Any religion that defies this new order, showing that it is unwilling to come into line with man's decrees, will soon find itself first cut out of the political arena and next out of the economic market. Society will scorn the truly righteous as bigots and inferior. Already in the United States, those who refuse to work on Sunday in order that they may worship are being passed over for employment. People who have no regard for a day of worship are being hired.

This is clearly the "woe" generation that calls "evil good and good evil." But are we to believe that in the midst of the "woes," God will remain silent? According to Joel and Peter, the louder Satan yells, the more God is going to speak to and through His people.

The Voice of Prophecy is Returning

Christian denominations that have not heard prophecy for hundreds of years should expect to have it return with unction and power. Visions, dreams, unusual spiritually-initiated events should be expected.

Paul and I were invited to hold a series of meetings in Connecticut at a Baptist church, where several Baptist ministers were in attendance each night. On the first night of the meetings, as the opening statements were being made by the host, God spoke to me to get down and roll across the front of the sanctuary as soon as he finished. Reluctantly I obeyed and then I stood up and said, "God instructed me to do that saying if I would roll on the floor He would roll in great power upon these meetings."

The pastor smiled and said, "I can't believe this. Only today one of my worship leaders said to me, 'I have a tremendous urge to roll on the floor.'"

Two days later that same pastor came to the service with one half of his mustache shaved off. Standing before his congregation he explained that God had instructed him to do this with the explanation that he and his people had been half-hearted in their commitment to Him. A time of repentance followed and every service was as God had promised—great with revival signs and wonders. God is speaking again to the Church today in a prophetic volume that is going to be hard to ignore.

One of the first things to change in our church when the revival came was our people's ability to hear from the Lord. Not that we hear as much as we should, or as much as we could if we were more attuned to God's ways, but we are hearing. Every worship service is blessed with some of the most eloquent and rich prophecies imaginable. Under the direction of the pastor, proven members of the body are allowed to exercise the gift of prophecy. Almost without fail, the theme of the sermon is announced in the prophecies, even though those prophesying have no idea what the message will be.

At one Wednesday morning service, surrounded by a sanctuary in the process of being expanded, our worship leader Susan began to sing the "Song of the Lord." This is a prophetically-inspired message set to music.   The message of the song was a call to "brokenness." A spoken word immediately followed the song with a call to "empty ourselves." As soon as this word was finished, a second member of the worship team began to sing the "Song of the Lord" concerning "rebuilding."   Susan followed with another refrain on "usefulness." A spoken word followed this song with the message of "transparency."

Following this prophetic antiphony, the Holy Spirit then moved to me and called attention to the sanctuary expansion the revival has necessitated.   Broken walls, exposed cables, carpet rolls, a broken stage all loomed before us. Then the word of the Lord came forth:

"Brokenness, emptying, rebuilding, usefulness, transparency. In order to expand, the old form must be broken down. There can be no revival unless there is a willingness to let go the old form and make room for something more. The satisfied are not hungry. Only the empty, the hungry, get blessed. Allow yourself to be broken by the Lord, emptied of all your strivings, stripped clean of all your bondages and sin.

Revival 2000!

> *"I will take the empty pieces of your life and rebuild you into a vessel of usefulness for the Lord. A vessel that is useful is one that has become transparent, one whose flesh no longer blocks the image of God. When people look at a transparent believer they see someone who has allowed the Holy Spirit to purge the heart until God shines through without compromise.*
>
> *"Revival is come that you may become one with the many-chambered God. There are rooms within the infinite God that man has yet to discover. The call has come to enter into God, into places with Him you never thought possible, to know Him and the power of His resurrection life!"*

Brokenness before God, empty of self, rebuilt by the Holy Spirit, useful for spiritual works, transparency with no flesh hindering our witness, this is the message God spoke to us that morning, yet in much greater detail than I can relate here. When the Holy Spirit speaks, He creates a spiritual sensitivity in the heart that allows God to be refreshingly personal with His people. The spoken messages of the Holy Spirit's ministry during worship melts the stoniest hearts, bringing us into scriptural wholeness.

The Family Attitude

Evidence of this wholeness at our church can be seen in the first program to be birthed out of our revival. By the fourth month of the outpouring of the Holy Spirit, a "Joy Ministry" was birthed to make sure every person who comes into our sanctuary feels welcome. We follow up each visit with a call of encouragement and invite them to refreshments and a time of fellowship. Those who accept this invitation are greeted by the pastor and made aware of the vision and opportunities in the church. We have finally begun to strengthen our commission to love. In part, this can all be traced back to a "family attitude" that is being developed during our prophecy-laced praise and worship.

The time has come for the Church to wake up. God is speaking. Evidence of His voice is breaking out in all kinds of expressions great and small. One sad young woman sat near the front row during an evening service, and I knew God was going to minister to her. When the opportunity came, she walked down to the front for prayer. Suddenly I saw, with the eye of the Spirit, a photograph that had a whole section faded. As I began to share this one-frame vision, the young woman fell on me and began weeping out loud.

I then saw praying hands forming the shape of a flower. "As you continue to pray, God is going to take that part of your life that has faded and He is going to cause it to blossom," I prophesied. We prayed together and a look of joy covered the young woman's face. The word was simple to me, but weighty to the woman. To have God love and encourage you in a very personal way is never trite or unimportant. Certainly this word was not like Ezekiel's visions, but it comforted her heart. She experienced the family attitude within our body of believers, and the power of genuine prophesy.

Pastor Paul gave an invitation to the congregation on a Sunday morning. "All who have a sharp or loose tongue, come down. God is going to minister to you." Among those who came was a young woman crying in great agony. After a few minutes I walked near and I could hear her saying, "Oh God, I've been so cruel to my mother. I've destroyed her with my sharp tongue. Oh God, it's not enough to say I'm sorry. I have to stop destroying my mother with my tongue!" Again, the touch of the family attitude brought through word of knowledge.

A Fresh Appreciation of the Gifts

A pastor, who had experienced excesses in prophecy, recently said to me, "I'm willing to listen about revival with signs following, but in truth, I cut out all prophecy in my church five years ago." Some churches cut it out four-hundred years ago or more. When John Calvin accepted Augustine's first works only, and not his latter writings, Calvin set the course for spiritually non-gifted, Protestant Christianity. It was Calvin who formulated the doctrine that the gifts of the Spirit ceased with the original apostles.

Augustine's writings from the fourth century A.D. had great influence on Christian doctrine, both Protestant and Catholic. Not until the last few years of his life, when so many people were healed that it forced attention, did Augustine take the gifts of the Holy Spirit seriously. He, too, had assumed that they passed with the death of the last apostle. Yet, after he discovered that God still heals, Augustine wrote three books correcting his error in doctrine. Both Calvin and Luther read Augustine's early writings, but unfortunately, neither one ever acknowledged Augustine's later books correcting the doctrinal errors of his earlier writings.

In spite of the contributions of these later writings toward recovering the fundamental truths of biblical faith, Protestant Christianity has been impoverished ever since with regard to wonderful the gifts of the Holy Spirit in the life of believers. Catholics who maintained belief in the supernatural, even though there have been excesses in some of their apparitions, have at times enjoyed supernatural healings more so than Protestants.

In his letter to the Church, Paul makes it clear that the gifts of the Holy Spirit are the manifestation of the innate abilities of the Spirit Himself. They are not learned, well-trained abilities of sincere believers (see 1 Cor. 12:7). Paul also reveals the fact that the grace gifts of the Holy Spirit are "*given to every man.*" That is to say, the Holy Spirit manifests Himself through ordinary people in the Church. To the natural eye, it looks as though "people" are prophesying; "people" are healing; "people" are giving tongues and interpretation (another form of prophecy); and "people" are performing miracles. Such is not the case. Manifestations of the Holy Spirit are initiated and performed by the Spirit himself, men are merely the channels or the conductors of spiritual "electricity." We transmit what God initiates.

Any believer is subject to being used of the Spirit to minister God's grace. But the people who **speak for God**, are people who have first been **spoken to by God**. For a minister to say that God is not speaking to His people today, and then purport to preach from the God's Word on His behalf, is preposterous. Israel had God's Word when they rejected Jesus. Without the ever-present work of the Holy Spirit, the Scriptures are impossible to personally appropriate—by the ordained minister or the layman.

> *"However, when He, the Spirit of truth, has come, He will guide you into all truth; for He will not speak on His own authority, but whatever He hears He will speak; and He will tell you things to come"* (John 16:13 NKJV).

One year before revival came to our church, God began to encourage us that a great move of His Spirit was coming. After the revival began and many were baffled by the supernatural manifestations suddenly occurring, words of prophecy began to come forth that said we were called to be "front runners," a "show case" for those God would bring. When no visitors had yet entered our church beyond the usual number, the Holy Spirit began to tell us that people would be coming from near and far, to see the things He was doing. Every word of what was spoken is being fulfilled weekly. From Uganda, England, Germany, India, Poland, Israel, the Far East, they are coming. Hardly a day goes by that we do not get more calls, asking, "Is the revival at your Church still in progress?"

"It's only intensifying," we respond.

"We'll be there!" They are coming just as the prophetic words announced. We were thrilled to hear an exciting report from England after a husband and wife in the ministry visited the revival at our church. Their letter, in part, follows:

Croydon, England October 3, 1994

Dear Paul and Mona:

BEYOND EXPECTATION!! Our first Sunday back from Boston, I shared during the evening service about the blessings we received from you. After I'd shared, I invited people forward. They came, and they fell under the power of the Holy Spirit as they came forward.

On Tuesday, we went to our leadership retreat and I shared about the revival. Before the end of the first day, we were all under the anointing of the Holy Spirit, and two mighty prophecies had come from my lips. I had explained to them that Mona had laid hands on me to receive the prophetic anointing. So they all realized this was an impartation of the gifting from the Lord!

John E. asked me to lay hands on all the elders for this prophetic gifting—and, Praise the Lord, many of them began to prophesy and continue to do so! The Lord has given me several personal prophecies also for various leaders. I said things my mind would not have thought of. . .(the following) general prophecy I spoke even thrilled me:

"For long years the people of the world have looked at the Church as a cold prison cell...a cold, uninviting, lonely

place...uncomfortable...joyless, unfurnished. They have looked through the iron bars in the windows and thought, If we join those people, we too will be trapped in a prison house of cold religion...but the Spirit says, 'Today is a day of transformation for the house of God.' The Spirit is furnishing the Church with wonderful things...it is becoming a place of beauty, of joy, of laughing, dancing, warmth, with deep love of one member for the other—it is becoming a place so desirable to be in, the people of the world will be drawn to its glorious experience. Multitudes will come into the Feast of good things!"

Yesterday morning I stood in for a preaching engagement and THE FIRE FELL!! They had to clear the chairs to the back of the room, push the communion table to a corner because people were falling down all over the place! I was ministering to them all for one and a half hours.

Last night I was back in New Life Christian Center. I wasn't preaching. In fact, no one preached last night...THE FIRE FELL!! Right at the beginning, I danced alone (to start with) across the front of the church. Honor joined me. We began to shout praises to God, and started waving to the people to come out and join us. Soon the whole front was filled with dancing people...just like at the CTWC. We cleared all the chairs in the center section of the auditorium. The leaders all began to minister to the people and soon there were hundreds and hundreds of bodies prostrate on the floor. People were grabbing me and saying, "Pray for me, I want what you've got!" The meeting went on for four and a half hours last night. It was mighty AWESOME!!

Revival has come to NLCC. The place was packed all day yesterday. Maybe 1,200 to 1,400 people have now been touched by the power of God on one day alone. I've heard that revival within the Church is continuing to extend here in England. At least 1,400 churches are experiencing the fresh anointing. So things are really happening here in our country as well as America, Canada and other nations.

David and Honor Lilley

Divinely Inspired Prophecy

We are well aware of the dangers of prophetic abuse, and we have taken every reasonable precaution to prevent "spiritual drifters" from using this very real stream of anointed prophecy to swim in at the expense of soundness. We know the traditional role of the Old Testament prophets who spoke the inspired Scriptures directly for God. We know that New Testament prophets have become spokesmen and spokeswomen with a degree of inspiration less than the God-breathed Scriptures, yet with more inspiration than a well-prepared sermon. We know the difference between the office of prophet in the Church and the gift of prophecy among the laity. But we also know that God said prophecy would increase, as the day of Jesus' return draws near.

Before the coming of Christ, divinely inspired prophecy will come from believers of every position in the congregation. It will come from both male and female, as it always has. Using Paul's analogy of the human body as the Church (1 Cor. 12), prophecy will come from the "foot," the "hand," the "eye," the "ear." God himself said:

"And it shall come to pass in the last days, saith God, I will pour out of my Spirit upon all flesh: and your sons and your daughters shall prophesy. . ." (Acts 2:17 KJV).

We know we are in the last days. John called it "the last time" (1 John 2:18). In these last days, prophecy will increase greatly. It has, in fact, been multiplying in the Church for the past two-hundred years, with an increasing acceleration. The time has come for the Church to catch up with "*the last time*."

The Weavings of God's Thoughts

The beloved, late Pastor of the Tenth Avenue Presbyterian Church, Dr. Donald Grey Barnhouse, once told the story of being in a little village in Belgium where he observed a handle loom. The host explained how the threads were placed first on the frame and then the shuttle moved back and forth over the threads, developing the material and creating the pattern that was in the mind of the weaver. Dr. Barnhouse wrote:

> "The principle which I saw demonstrated in that loom was in the mind of the Holy Spirit when He inspired some of the sacred writers to express the idea of thoughts. *'For my thoughts are not your thoughts, neither are your ways my ways, saith the Lord'* (Isa. 55:8). The word which is here translated 'thoughts' means literally 'weavings.' My weavings are not your weavings. Everywhere in Scripture, we are face to face with the absolute difference between God and man in all of God's ways of thinking and doing." (*Let Me Illustrate*, Dr. Donald Gray Barnhouse, Revell, pg. 134).

When God speaks who will not listen, regardless how different or unusual the weavings may be?

10

Stop Whining and Start Burning

Any minister who really listens to the people who come for prayer and counseling would have to admit that he needs help beyond himself. The sadness and depression in the Church today is formidable. The phrases one often hears are heartbreaking: "My husband died—my wife left me—my children turned against me—five years, ten years, twenty years ago—I've cried every day since."

Grief is normal, and a reasonable amount is even healing and healthy. But any grief that runs into years, molding the griever's whole life around his or her loss, is not of God. The Bible tells us clearly that we, should ". . . *sorrow not, even as others which have no hope*" (1 Thess. 4:13 KJV). If we are not careful, what starts out as valid grief ends up in self-pity and whining. We cry on every available shoulder until we become totally bound up in our losses and God is no longer any consolation or joy to us.

God values valid tears and makes a record of them—tears of reasonable sadness, of repentance, of love, of thanksgiving, of joy, and certainly those shed over the lost. But God has taught me something in this fresh anointing: Some people feel they are more likely to get

God's attention if they cry than if they laugh and praise Him! This is not true, for God is inviting His people to walk out of their depression and tears through the many exit doors He is providing in this revival.

Exit doors from depression? Yes, through praise and worship. Singing, clapping our hands, dancing, laughing and shouting can all drive depression far from us. Total investment of ourselves in praise and worship will release our mind and emotions from the burdens they are carrying, even though you may say, "But when I stop praising, the burdens are still there."

And they may be. If you have problems that need attention when you begin to worship, they will probably still need attention when you are through. But total liberty in praise will increase your ability to handle the burdens. Your vision will be clearer. Your perspective of things will be more balanced, and a new flow of God's wisdom within your spirit will provide a better solution.

No parents like for their children to whine. How many times have we said so to our own offspring? "Will you please stop whining!" Whining tends to irritate human parents. I don't know if whining irritates God or not, but I do know that whining never brings His favor. Trusting Him and giving Him praise is the attitude that brings down the power. This revival is calling the Church to take a more joyful approach to its problems. Faith in God and despair over natural circumstances certainly send a mixed signal to God and to those who are watching you. Joy under fire makes the good witness and pleases God immensely.

Joy Under Fire

After nine months into this present revival, I was enjoying abundant happiness when all of a sudden an old anxiety hit the core of my soul. I found myself going back thirty years trying to figure out why I handled a certain, painful situation the way I did. I began to relive and try to sort out something I have never fully understood. Soon a voice from that sick feeling in the pit of my stomach said, "How can you go out now and talk about revival when your joy is gone? How can you tell people that God is bringing refreshing into the Church when your refreshing didn't last?"

I knew right off it sounded like Satan, but the blanket of misery that dropped over my mind was too heavy to shrug off. I began to pray and pour out my soul before God in a literally mind-scraping experience that took me past every idol of pride and ambition I had left standing. I was left with nothing but my conversion at seven years of age. "But what did I understand at that age?" I questioned even of that. "How could a seven-year-old child really encounter God?"

For some time I was tossed back and forth in the spiritual realm until I said "Lord, you called me at a young age for the precise reason that I had nothing to offer you but 'yes.' You saved me at seven the same way you save people at seventy—all by yourself." Salvation is not based on what we do or do not comprehend doctrinally or theologically. It is not what we have done that is bad, or what we shall do that is good. When God saves a soul, He does it His way and He does it alone.

Almighty God alone foreordains our lives, just as He alone breathed us into existence. Then He alone searched us out of five billion people and opened our hearts to repent of sin and agree that He was Lord. He alone restored our souls to fellowship with Him. Alone, He put the will in us and anointed us to serve Him. The truth is, there was never anything we could offer but "yes." He alone did the rest.

Revival is a time to glory. But God is setting the record straight. It is no credit to ourselves that God pours out His Spirit upon us. By the counsel of His own will, God sees the dried and waste areas of people's lives and He pours in the "oil and the wine." Anointed and intoxicated by His Spirit, we are each poured out into the world and revival does its work.

I came out of my encounter with anxiety with no medals, for none were due me. But whatever medals or accolades I did find, I quickly pinned onto the worthy shoulder that carried the cross for my sins. My joy returned and, in humility and gratitude, I continue spreading the knowledge of revival. Jesus did not promise the disciples any medals for going out and fulfilling the Great Commission. He just said to them:

> *"Behold, I give you the authority to trample on serpents and scorpions, and over all the power of the enemy, and nothing shall by any means hurt you. Nevertheless do not rejoice in this, that the spirits are subject to you, but rather rejoice because your names are written in heaven"* (Luke10:19,20 NKJV).

Was the anxiety attack from Satan? Probably, but what is unusual about that? I have people coming to me regularly to say, "I'm having to fight all over again. Is something wrong with me?"

I tell them, "No, Satan's just repeating his pattern. He only left Jesus alone for a season and then he came right back. Keep fighting!"

God does do a deeper cleansing in us during times of battle and He refocuses our attitudes. Give glory to God for His miraculous works in our midst, but remember that our relationship with Him is always, first and foremost, our greatest blessing.

Revival is For Those Who Wish to be Revived

This revival is for every nation, people, culture and tongue. Orthodox, Catholic and Protestant alike are targeted by the Spirit, regardless of tradition. God wants to come into the midst of all His people to comfort and empower them, and all who hunger for more of Him will certainly be fed more. Yet, I will not sit in condemnation of those who refuse to enter in. In humility, I will eat my portion and be grateful. This is what God worked into my soul while He reminded me of my own most treasured blessing—that I know Him. Without minimizing His blessings or missing out on them, to know Him is itself the soul's greatest reward.

The Church does not need revival to enhance the fact of their blessed regeneration (the new birth). The blood of Jesus completely saves and God left nothing out. The Church does, however, need to be periodically refreshed in its intimacy with God to have the power, the vision and the anointing to go out into the world and effectively share this great salvation with those who have yet to receive it.

Some of our people have become annoyed with each other as God has manifested himself in various ways. "He laughs too loudly—she always falls out in the Spirit—the dancing is too fleshy—the prophecy is too long—the shouting is too piercing!" Perhaps the Spirit needs to baptize the Christian crankiness out of all of us a little bit more.

It reminds me of my first summer camp. Because I couldn't swim, my mother forbid me to go into the water. But what was summer camp if I couldn't get into that wonderful water where everybody was having so much fun? My brother and I headed for the creek that summer to teach me to swim. Within two weeks I could "dog paddle" well enough to assure my mother I wouldn't drown, and off to camp we went. After a few days of polishing my skills, the counselors announced a swimming meet. Novice that I was, I entered. On the day of the race, all of the contestants stood at one end of the pool. When the whistle blew, I hit a "belly buster," stuck my head up out of the water and began to paddle with all my might. At that point my brother, who was standing on the sideline, had one of two options. He could criticize my terrible style or he could applaud my efforts and encourage me on.

So long as I live, I will never forget that greatest of all swimming meets. Fighting the water like an enemy, I was giving everything a twelve-year old can give when I heard my brother following along the side screaming, "Go on, Mona, keep fighting. You're doing good!" That year I went home bursting with pride and a red satin ribbon that said that, in spite of my poor form, I had won second place among twelve contestants.

Is God only moving in people's lives if their performance is polished and to our natural liking? Who knows how our natural performance actually looks to the eyes of a Holy God? During times of worship and ministry, the movings of the Spirit are usually expressed through the personalities and abilities of the people just as they are. Bad voices usually stay unpleasant to the natural ear. Loud voices rarely become soft. Tall people may look awkward. Short people may look like a part of the carpet design. But flesh is responding to the real presence of the living God and it shows.

Demonstrations of the Spirit are not "people performances." This is one reason why those who are being touched do not look physically polished. There have been no rehearsals. When God moves, men usually look astonished or something other than "in control." When God moves, men are not in fact in control. God is.

A legal secretary who commands a good salary has been in our church for years. She is the epitome of neatness and organization. When the revival came to our church, this "in control" young woman fell to the floor and began to quietly shake her head and body back and forth. Some would question if that was a result of God's presence enveloping her. My response is, "She never did it before." The young woman says she understands what God is doing during these encounters.

Physical responses to unrehearsed surges of divine power come in unusual ways. Some people shake, some cry, some laugh, some hop up and down like popcorn popping. But none of those who are significantly touched by God just sit quietly as though nothing was happening. Some complain the unusual behavior is "excessive," but I say it is a human "expression" of the influence of the Spirit. And since it is in response to God and not to man, it would take God to say whether or not it is too much.

When God Speaks

When my first book on revival, *"The Fresh Anointing,"* was published, I mailed a copy to my mother. Considering her 83 years in Scripture, I always appreciate her comments. A few days after I mailed the book, however, I left for Latvia to spread the revival. Two days after I returned from my trip, her call came, "Your new book is the best yet! Especially the subject of joy."

According to my mother, "About fifty years ago, the little Methodist church we were attending held revival meetings. The visiting minister preached a sermon entitled, 'Here's the Well, but Where's the Rope and Bucket?' It was one of the best messages we had ever heard. People in the community talked about it for months. And now, fifty years later, your book answers that very question the best way I've ever read. It's with joy that we draw water from the wells of salvation! Isaiah agreed with my mother: *'Therefore with joy you will draw water from the wells of salvation'* (Isa. 12:3 NKJV)."

When Jesus told the infamous woman (with five husbands) at the well that He would give her such water that she would never thirst again, He did not mean spiritual thirst would cease. Jesus was telling her that He had a water that would cure her thirst for this world. He always made it clear that it is right to thirst for more of the Spirit. *"Blessed are those who hunger and thirst for righteousness, for they shall be filled"* (Matt. 5:6 NKJV).

We made one exhausting trip to share this revival with a minister who invited us to come and let them see what was happening. After four days and twenty hours of visible manifestations of the Holy Spirit, the minister said, "No, this revival is not for this culture."

How did his congregation respond? They drank like thirsty people on a desert march. They laughed and shouted all over the place. I watched a young woman whose husband had recently been let out of prison grab hold the power of the "hallelujah shout." Her piercing voice literally shot forth like an arrow in every service. But the pastor seemed completely unimpressed with everything, for he was not thirsty. He seemed choked on satisfaction with his present vision. His passion for what he was doing appeared to be more important to him than the greater thing God wanted to bring about in his work through a fresh anointing.

The Record

I am committed to refraining from judging any brother or sister in the Lord concerning revival, yet I will plead the record of history. During the Great Awakening of the 1730s and 40s, a scholarly Yale pastor named Jonathan Edwards and a Harvard minister named Charles Chauncy battled each other for the life of the revival. Perhaps neither of these two men realized the future impact their opposing positions would have on the lives of millions of souls to follow.

Both scholars wrote books on the awakening. Chauncy's *"Seasonable Thoughts on the State of Religion in New England"* was a detailed refutation of Edwards' defense of the awakening called *"Some Thoughts Concerning Revival."* Chauncy's book was released in 1743 and became an instant best-seller. Edwards' book sold slowly with only one printing during his lifetime. According to William DeArteaga, "It took several generations to recognize it [Edwards' work] as a classic of discernment and psychology of spiritual experiences."

Given time, the course of Charles Chauncy's life took him into a theology of universal salvation—salvation for all men, the trinity quickly discarded and the deity of Jesus Christ replaced with Unitarianism. Mr. DeArteaga's recorded these words:

> "Here lies the true fruit of Chauncy's opposition to the awakening. A theology of the Spirit is difficult to maintain if one rejects the presence of the Holy Spirit during revival when His work is most manifest. The third person of the trinity becomes a doctrine without verification and easily reasoned away" (Quenching the Spirit, pgs. 52,53).

The Spirit of God cannot be quenched without serious consequences. Charles Chauncy saved face among his colleagues of the 1700s by calling the Holy Spirit's move emotionalism and radical. That was the easy way out, for it required no change, no challenge, no adjustments. Jonathan Edwards on the other hand suffered great rejection for several years. Held up to the light of their moment, Chauncy won by a wide margin. His writings caused sufficient controversy to offend the Holy Spirit and stop The Great Awakening at the time.

Given further time, however, a call was extended to Jonathan Edwards to become the president of Princeton University, and today his works are still respected for their keen insight into spiritual experience. Chauncy's work is seen for what it was—opposition from an apostate spirit that ultimately denied the deity of Christ.

A call came to our office that a mega-church had recently come out against this present revival. I felt sad. It is one thing to turn away from flow, it is another to challenge it. Remembering Edwards and Chauncy, however, I knew I would rather lose face among my colleagues now and have history prove me wise than to be among those who failed miserably to discern the hour of their visitation.

Time to Catch Fire

John Wesley said, "Get on fire for God and men will come just to watch you burn." People are coming to watch us burn at Christian Teaching and Worship Center, and many are catching the fire themselves!

It is time that the Church stop whining and start burning, stop pretending to believe in Pentecost and start blazing with Pentecostal liberty. God is not going to draw a crowd to hear people who only talk about what God used to do. It is time the Church stopped pretending to believe in a living Christ, when they cry "radicalism" every time He starts to move among them.

The world has arrived at a dark period, and the Church must go into action. Light is always radiated out from energy in action. This revival is energizing God's people, giving them boldness and liberty, to step out in ways of witnessing and testifying that they have never before thought they could do. And the powerful light of Jesus Christ is radiating out from their efforts.

Testimony of Beth—August 11, 1994

"God has ministered to me through a miracle which took place in our church on Monday evening, August 1st, when He restored the sight of a woman who had been legally blind. The following morning, as I was commuting to work on the train and reading my Bible, I began to reflect on the awesomeness of what God had done the night before. It really was incredible!

"Then the Holy Spirit began to impress me to share the news of what had happened. I decided to share this exciting news with my two closest co-workers. But the Holy Spirit said, *'Share it further.'* As I walked through Boston Common towards my place of work, I thought, Okay, I'll share with the entire office. Then the Holy Spirit said, *'That's good, Beth, but I want you to start with that woman walking ahead of you.'* My flesh began to rise up, and I thought, Oh no! A stranger!

"For a few moments, I battled fear, possible rejection and humiliation. But the Holy Spirit pressed in so strongly that I knew if I didn't speak to that woman, I would regret it. Never before had I stopped a perfect stranger and shared my faith. So I began to tell this stranger what I had witnessed the night before, encouraging her that Jesus is alive and if she had a need, He would meet it.   The encounter lasted only a few seconds, and her reaction was a mixture of surprise and fear. I did not know how or if those words would minister to that woman, that was up to God. I was just obedient and spreading the news. And I have not stopped. That was just the beginning.

"Shortly after I arrived at work I had to run an errand. As I was leaving, I saw two young men sitting at a sidewalk cafe just outside my building. They appeared to be construction workers having a coffee break. As I passed by, the Holy Spirit told me to share the news with them. I fought and argued, No, Lord, please. Not those two! I told myself that this really wasn't the Holy Spirit, I was just getting carried away. So I passed them by and kept walking. Never would I choose to approach two young men who would probably think I am crazy.

"Again, the Holy Spirit pressed in so much that I had to turn around. My flesh was burning, but I approached them anyway and shared the miracle. One of them responded that he had said his rosary that morning. I said, 'Don't pray to your rosary, pray to the One who saves! Pray to the One who heals!' As I returned from my brief errand, the Lord directed me to say another word of encouragement to these two men. I was hoping they would be gone, but they were not. As I began to pass by, I said, 'Remember, Jesus will meet your need!'

"Surprisingly, they called me over to ask me some questions. One said, 'Well, you picked the right people to tell. I believe you.'

"Through the healing which took place that night, God has put a boldness in me that I would not have believed possible. He has set me free! Every day I share the miracle with strangers on the train, or sitting on a bench in Boston Public Garden. Even when I go out jogging in the morning, I will call out to whomever I pass as I jog down the street, 'I witnessed a miracle, Jesus is still healing today, Hallelujah!' And I know that three months from now I will have new miracles to witness about.

"In setting me free, God has also shown me what true joy is. The more people I share with, the more joy I feel. I began to realize that my joy really is in serving Him. As if to confirm this for me, a few days after I began to witness, a friend called me at work with some news that made me very, very sad. I walked to the train feeling downhearted. As I sat on the train, I thought, Oh Lord, is it okay if I take a break from sharing just for a little while? I'm feeling very sad and I just want to gather in and collect myself. That's all right, isn't it?

"'No,' spoke the Spirit, *'tell the two women sitting next to you.'* But Lord, I just don't feel that exuberant right now, I protested. *'Tell them anyway.'* I leaned over towards the two women and began to share the miracle. Immediately I was flooded with joy! I knew for certain that my joy is not in anything of this world. It is not in a marriage partner, it is not in children, in a job or even a dream home—my joy is in the Lord and serving Him. No matter what my circumstances, I truly understand what it means to say, *'The joy of the Lord is my strength.'* Serving God gives me joy, and the joy gives me strength!"

Crawling for Jesus

During our annual celebration of the Feast of Tabernacles, I was standing in front of a packed house. Visitors from many places came to join us for Succot and to pray for Israel. Near the end of one of the services, our guest speaker was drawing to a close when I felt the Holy Spirit saying to me, *"Get down and crawl to the front of the altar. When you get there, stand and say, 'Many of you are asking how you can enter into this revival. You may enter in as a little child—coming to God with child-like faith and humility.'"*

I began to pray. If this is what God wanted, I was willing to humble myself before the people and crawl to the altar. But, in the natural, I really wanted to be sure it was God. I waited for the guest speaker to finish his message, and he concluded his message with an invitation which immediately filled the altar. Relieved, I thought about this word over the next few weeks.

On a following Sunday morning, a very quiet and unassuming woman in our congregation suddenly broke loose and began dancing. I had never before seen her caught up in the presence of God to any great extent. All of a sudden, this same woman fell to her knees and crawled quickly all the way down the main aisle of the sanctuary! She then jumped up and danced all the way back up the aisle in a wonderful liberty I have rarely seen. Did her flesh burn? Perhaps. But her light was radiant!

One month later, a minister I knew was visiting our church for the first time. I wanted to make a good impression on him about the soundness of this revival. As the worship advanced, I ended up at the back of the church ministering to people. The Holy Spirit suddenly swept over me and I fell under the power beside an airline pilot. After a few minutes, I heard the Spirit say, "Get up and crawl down the aisle to the front." This time I obeyed quickly.

After the service, we were greeting the visitors when a young woman came up to me and said, "I was sitting in your service this morning, and I was quite skeptical. I said to myself, 'Their clothes are too fine and they are filled with pride.' But then I saw you crawling down the aisle and I knew I was wrong." Through one simple act of obedience, God rewove her thinking.

Obedience to God is always the one key we can use to open the barred doors of fear, doubt and pride. Through our obedience to His outpouring, He is reweaving all our unrenewed, miserable thought processes and we are being set free!

11

Life-Changing Worship

The anointing we are experiencing during worship at the Christian Teaching and Worship Center is life changing. Two young women recently visited our church for the first time. They walked into the foyer, then looked very startled when they peered into the sanctuary where people were joyously worshipping. "We're not going in there!" they said and ran out. But after "regrouping," they came back into another section of the building and entered the sanctuary through a side door. Before the service was over, these two young women had been saturated in the presence of God. Three days later, they called the church and said, "We are still drunk in the Spirit! We have never experienced anything like this before! Our whole family has been invaded!"

The Holy Spirit is God's agent of communication for the Church, as Jesus made very clear on several different occasions in the Scriptures. The Spirit is definitely speaking through worship today. Let us always remember that Jesus said several times, *"He that hath ears to hear, let him hear what the Spirit saith unto the churches."*

In June of 1994, at a conference we were holding in Topsham, Maine, we opened our Saturday morning session with music. As the praise began to flow the Holy Spirit began to give me fresh insight into worship, and I got up and shared what had been spoken to me. The music resumed and then I received further development of the message. This exchange between music and insight went on for an hour. Since the service was being taped, I asked for a copy of that unusual hour. What had happened during that period of time was definitely not "ordinary" and I wanted to hear what the Spirit had to say. The following is the sermon that was imparted to us that morning. I believe it describes the true worshiper, the one whom Jesus said worships *"in spirit and in truth."*

THE PROPHETIC MESSAGE

Worship Through Physical Expression

God can only be worshipped in Spirit. We can discipline our minds to bow to His Spirit, but we can never worship Him mentally. *"God is a Spirit: and they that worship him must worship him in spirit and in truth"* (John 4:24 KJV). A physical expression of worship—dancing, clapping, shouting—may disturb some of the people, but worship is for the eyes of God, not for the eyes of man. The Lord does not look on the outside; He looks within the heart to see what is motivating the expression. Only God can judge what is given to Him.

Who among men can judge the amount of physical expression due Him? Even if the body is made to look foolish to the natural mind, would this hinder the God who is looking within? The body is a temple of the Holy Spirit designed to serve worship, so clearly God does not view our bodies in the same we do. The external structure of temple buildings do not worship, it is always the people inside the temples who worship. Physical expression during worship is simply physical responses to the spirit within, as it flows with the Spirit of God. Singing, clapping, dancing is a physical response to the Spirit.

If your hands are filled with the Spirit, why wouldn't they reach out to God? If your feet are filled with the Spirit, why wouldn't they leap and dance? If your mouth and heart are filled with the Spirit and your voice and your vocal cords are touched with the Spirit, why wouldn't they bring forth loud praises to God? It is the spirit man within that is being released.

Physical expression that flows with the Holy Spirit is appropriate, it is biblical and it is pleasing in God's sight. Total worship—body, soul and spirit—is glorious praise unto God. So do not be inhibited. Take the message out to all, that we worship in the Spirit the God who is Spirit.

During worship, discipline your body to do whatever it has to do in order to allow your spirit to express what the Holy Spirit is calling you to express. If the Holy Spirit is moving upon your spirit to leap, then leap; if it is to yell, then yell; if it is to sing and clap, then sing and clap; if it is to fall to the floor, then fall. Respond in your spirit man to the Holy Spirit and you will cause your body to come into obedience to the Spirit's desires.

The Apostle Paul said, "*I keep under my body, and bring it into subjection. . .*" (1 Cor. 9:27 KJV). The Church needs to bring its body and its mind under the will of the Holy Spirit. Our bodies are designed to become obedient to the Spirit of God. We should not be ashamed to publicly submit our physical temple to His holy will. God says:

"All the earth is mine. All creation and all beings—all life, all sound and all movement. What will I not lay claim to? What should not be open and free to worship Me? What do I not own? What is not mine? What should not be allowed to

freely, joyfully, wholly worship me? All things contain life drawn from me, the source of life. What should I not lay claim to? What should not worship me abundantly, liberally, generously, loudly, softly, quietly, publicly? All the airwaves are mine. What airwaves should I not lay claim to? All things are mine. All praise belongs to me, all worship."

A Prayer of Surrender

Lord, we offer to you our bodies, our minds, our spirits. They are yours, Father, for you gave them and they do not belong to us. They are loans from you. They are not ours to do with as we please. We renounce the lie that tells us our bodies are ours to do with as we please. Murder and destruction of life (abortion) is the end result of that thing. We renounce that lie over this generation. We renounce that lie over the face of the earth. Man's body does not belong to him. The natural body is a house built by the mighty God, given to us, loaned to us, as a temple that belongs to Him.

All places of worship belong to God. False gods have crept in, but houses of worship belong to God. Our bodies are temples. We belong to you, Lord God. Take our bodies. Our sicknesses would not be so many if we truly realized our bodies are yours, and we released them totally to praise and worship. Jesus, help us to surrender what does not even belong to us. We surrender our bodies to you. They need strength, they need energy. Take them and repair them, Lord, they are yours. Let them be useful for your glory. You are the One in charge of the maintenance of our lives.

Teach us how to treat our physical temples. They are precious and valuable loans, these houses from you. Take our mind and spirit, wash them in your Word, wash them by Your Spirit. Clean out all wrong thinking, that we may behold the Holy God Yahweh in His most holy place. So we may know what it is like to enter into your glorious presence, Lord, let every shred of religion fall away from us and let true spirituality come forth.

Seated With Christ

We surrender our minds. Renew and renovate our minds that they will bow to the Spirit, that you may be all and all in our lives. Let your holy presence descend upon each one of us. Let us enter into places we have not walked before, that Jesus may become real to us. Lord, we want to walk in the heavenly realms with you.

Lord Jesus, lift us up to spiritual works, that fruit may come from our lives and that the works of our hands may be multiplied and prosperous and productive. Let all fear drain out of us and be washed away. Let only fear of God, reverence and respect for His will and ways remain.

Availability

We sometimes speak about climbing the steps of a ladder to heaven as though it were something we do. But the ladder to heaven is gained by round after round of surrender. Surrender and surrender and surrender. Glory is achieved only through surrender.

We surrender to you. We surrender our bodies, our minds, our finances, our homes, our children, our partners, our jobs, our professions, our businesses, our lands, our goods, our time. Availability comes only in surrender. It may be promised, but it is not available unless it is fully surrendered. Lord, we surrender all that you have given us. Our image, our reputation, we surrender. Our ethnic traditions, our religious tradition, we surrender. Our positions of authority and power in the earth, we surrender. We surrender it all back to you, Father.

We may think we are fully available, but there is much more availability within us. Father, let your fire fall on us and burn us free so that we are fully available. This is the secret the saints of old knew. All that they possessed was fully surrendered and fully available. Mighty exploits come from those fully surrendered and fully available. Work in us also and help us to fully surrender and become fully available. We give all and hold back nothing, as Jesus held nothing back.

Amen.

The Divine Exchange

Bless the wonderful name of Him who gave up all rights and position in all of heaven and of all that He possessed on earth. This is the pattern of the ministry and the message of Jesus. This is the Gospel. He surrendered all, holding nothing back. He gave all of heaven to earth, and He gave all of earth to heaven. This is the Father's divine pattern. All that God gives to you from heaven, give out to those around you. All that you have from the earth, give to Him. This is the divine exchange between heaven and earth.

When we give up all of our vision for all of God's vision, then we are going to see with the eyes of the Spirit. If we are eager and hungry and desperate and thirsty for the spiritual things, we will let go. Things are being released and sliding from our grasp as though they have been oiled, and they have been—by the Holy Spirit! Let even the flesh slide off from our bones that we may become totally transparent, holding onto nothing of our own. Flesh is sliding off and we are becoming the basic framework that the Father blew breath into. And that structure, that part of us that was created in His image, is coming forth to resurrection!

The Divine Image

The divine image is the structure God is bringing forth. This is the refreshing that is occurring in the Church today. Flesh is being humbled and made to appear foolish as God's eternal image is coming forth within those who are obedient. The eternal image is coming forth in the Church of the Lord Jesus Christ, and men are going to see visions because heaven is going to be opened to the spiritual man God is bringing forth. Men are going to dream dreams because heaven is going to be opened. Heaven and earth are coming together and blending into one. This is the divine exchange.

The mystery of Jesus Christ, that He was fully human and He was fully God, is coming to light in the Church. There is a merger taking place between heaven and earth, and the people of God are going to live in the image of God. What God does is going to be done in the people who are like Him, and even now it is coming across the face of the earth.

This divine merger is going to put cracks and crevices in the intellect of man, and men are going to put their hands on their brow and say, "What on earth is taking place?" The divine merger! The divine image from heaven is coming forth in the Church still here on earth. The religious image and all religiosity will bow down at the feet of Jesus and be washed away, that the true spirit man may come forth.

Let Us Bow the Knee

Worship in Spirit and in truth. Live and speak in Spirit and in truth. Then the power will be manifested in Spirit and in truth, and in reality. Then will great signs and wonders be done. Thank you, Lord Jesus, for what you are doing. How magnificent are your ways. Who could conceive, who could imagine such a plan that heaven and earth would merge together? Hallelujah!

Let us now bow on our knees before the Lord, especially those who have never bowed before Him. God is calling us to humble ourselves under His mighty hand. Worship on your knees before the Lord. Let us lay our all before our Lord, once and for all. He paid the price, once and for all. Let us give our all, once and for all.

Satan's Deception

When Jesus came down to earth, the devil came and tempted Him. He said, "Do not make this divine exchange. Let me give you all the power and glory of this present world."

But Jesus said, *"No, I will take the divine exchange. All of heaven I gave for earth. All of earth I will give for heaven. Anything less is not the divine way."* If we hold onto one tiny thing, then we are holding back the divine exchange. We must give all of heaven for all of earth and all of earth for all of heaven. We cannot hold back one thing.

Satan hoped to deceive Jesus, to persuade Him to hold back from the Father. Jesus could have said, "It is really mine, anyway. I created this earth." But He said, *"No, I'll hold nothing back. Father, you want me to give up heaven, I give up heaven. Father, you want me to give up earth, I give up earth."*

People of God, the way of God is surrender. Everyday, everything, every way, surrender all to the Father. Hallelujah!

Let My People Go!

Pastors, evangelists, church fathers, ecclesiastical hierarchy—surrender the Church! They are God's people. You have been appointed as overseer, not owner. If God's move removes people from your oversight, then you must be willing to let go. God's will is more important than numbers.

All leaders and heads of state, surrender the nations. These are God's nations. God will not allow us to hold one thing back from Him. He who called Abraham to offer Isaac says, *"Let go of your Isaac."* Everything you are, everything you possess, must become a living sacrifice or the divine exchange will not occur.

The Altar

The first thing to be established by God after the fall of man was the altar, and it will forever be present in God's economy. There must always be a place where you can surrender all to God, for there will never be a time when you will not be required to surrender. There will never be anything in your life that need not be surrendered to God. All must go on the altar and all must be consumed by the living God. *"For our God is a consuming fire"* (Heb. 23:29 KJV).

His is the fire that falls on a sacrifice on the altar. The fire does not fall on that which you keep for yourself—the fire falls on what you lay on the altar as sacrifice. Sacrifice everything, and then the fire will fall and God will consume and be pleased and leave a blessing.

The Beauty of God

The beauty of God has been lost to this generation. God is rarely worshipped for who He is. But God is restoring a spirit of worship in the Church. People are going to come together for hours at the time just to worship and be in His presence. Many will lie for hours basking in His goodness, and great will be the transformation of their lives. The sick will be restored, the grieving will find fresh joy, ministries will be birthed, the lost will find new birth.

The Great Commission

This is the great commission in demonstration through the saints by the witness of the Holy Spirit:

"Go ye into all the world and preach the Gospel to every creature. He that believeth and is baptized shall be saved . . ." (Mark 16:15-16 KJV).

We pray for the movings of the power of God among the nations. We pray that everywhere we go, the Good News of salvation will burn within our souls as never before. We are just beginning. Revival is just beginning. Pastors, it is just beginning. Ministers, it is just beginning. God's glory is going to be manifest on this earth and we are just beginning to enter in. We are just beginning. Hallelujah!

Cindy—healed and on fire!

Susan—Worship Leader
Spiritual intoxication

Life-Changing Worship

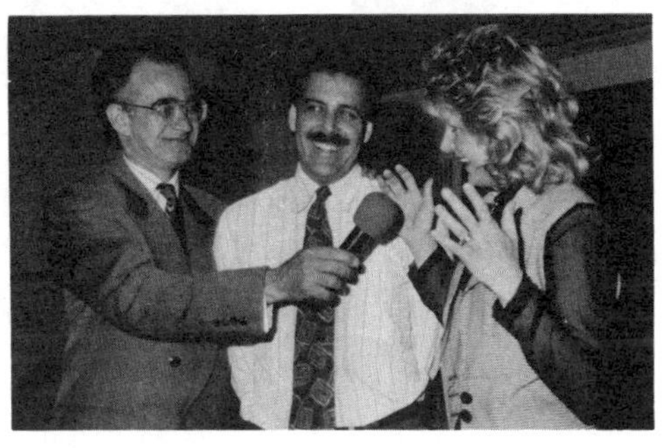

Tom and Donna—More than 150 salvations!

"Confirming the Word with signs following..."
(Spirit-initiated illustrations of truth)

Mona Johnian—Pour everything out before Him.

Steven—pianist at the Boston Ballet—Joy!

Pastor Paul—Come as a little child.

Virginia—aligning your walk with the Word.

The miracle baby!

Chapter 12

Hallelujah!

The Church is totally dependent on the Holy Spirit to have any contact with Christ. He is our guide, the One who speaks to us and leads us in all things concerning Christ. We can never quench the Holy Spirit and expect to know Christ better. In fact, we cannot even know Christ at all unless the Spirit reveals Him to us.

When the Spirit of God begins to move in special ways upon the earth, it is a call to drop everything that stands in the way of our full cooperation with what He is doing. Present programs, worship service formats, church calendars, annual events—everything should bow and if need be, move out of the way for the fresh direction of God's Spirit. He is here to reveal Jesus to us, and who in the Church has priority over Christ?

Father, Son and Spirit are all three equally Spirit, equally God and equally invested in the program of God on this earth. Whatever One does, all do. Whenever One is worshipped, all are worshipped. When One receives praise, all are glorified. Whenever One performs, all perform. God is Spirit, Christ is Spirit who took a flesh body (which He still retains in a glorified state) and the

Holy Spirit is Spirit. Father, Christ and the Holy Spirit are equally Spirit and equally God.

> *"There are three that bear witness in heaven, the Father, the Word, and the Holy Ghost: and these three are one"* (1 John 5:7 KJV).

Because of man's competitive nature and bent toward jealousy, we cannot comprehend perfect equality—divine equality. It is interesting that many people are afraid of revival because they fear an overemphasis of one aspect of God and diminution of the other, such as the Holy Spirit outshining the Father or the Son. In reality, this is the same as saying. "I'm afraid God is going to replace God."

One Godhead

In Matthew 28:19 (NKJV), Jesus makes no distinction among the Trinity when He says, *"Go therefore and make disciples of all the nations, baptizing them in the name of the Father and of the Son and of the Holy Spirit."* Actually, each personality of the Godhead is called God in various places in the Scriptures.

In Romans 1:7, Paul calls God *"our Father."*

In John 20:28, Thomas calls Jesus *"My Lord and my God."*

In Acts 5:3-4 (NKJV), Peter declared to Ananias that the Holy Spirit is God, when he said: *"Why has Satan filled your heart to lie to the Holy Spirit....You have not lied to men but to God."*

Creation came into existence through the Trinity: *"In the beginning God created the heavens and the earth...and the Spirit of God moved upon the face of the waters..."* (Gen. 1:1-2 KJV). This establishes the Father and the Spirit at creation. And then Paul establishes Jesus at the creation, *". . . The mystery, which from the beginning of the world hath been hid in God, who created all things by Jesus Christ"* (Eph. 3:9 KJV).

Father, Christ and Holy Spirit gave birth to creation and to the plan of saving creation. They alone are the power by which transactions between heaven and earth are accomplished. Men, creatures and nature are vehicles through which God moves, but everything God does is a spiritual transaction.

According to Jesus, the final and present program of restoring all creation back to the Father is being carried out on this earth by the person of the Holy Spirit:

> *"However, when He, the Spirit of truth, has come, He will guide you into all truth; for He will not speak on His own authority, but whatever he hears He will speak; and He will tell you things to come. He will glorify Me, for He will take of what is Mine and declare it to you. All things that the Father has are Mine. Therefore I said that He will take of Mine and declare it to you"* (John 16: 13-15 NKJV).

When the Spirit moves, Jesus is revealed. When Jesus is revealed, God is glorified.

Hallelujahs!

A key word that continues to be shouted in our worship services now is "Hallelujah!" The Spirit is lifting this word out of the dust of human programs and giving it back to God's people. Since revival has come to our church, throughout the week the hallways throughout our building ring with "Hallelujahs!" It's a weapon in our hands that paralyzes Satan. *"The praises of God's people still the avenger"* (Ps. 8:2 paraphrased).

Let us take a look at this word "hallelujah" and see what God has given us. Hallelujah is a compound word of three parts:

Revival 2000!

Hall—Hail
El—God the strong One, the Creator
Jah—Jehovah the Redeemer
Hail to God the Creator, and to Jehovah the Redeemer!
The first "hallelujah" in the Old Testament is found in Psalm 104:35 (NKJV): *"May sinners be consumed from the earth, and the wicked be no more. Bless the Lord, O my soul! Praise the Lord* [Hallelujah]!" The Talmud and the Midrash call attention to the fact that it is connected with the overthrow of the wicked.

The first "hallelujah" in the New Testament is also connected with judgment on the wicked: *"And after these things I heard a loud voice of a great multitude in heaven, saying, 'Alleluia! Salvation and glory and honor and power to the Lord our God! For true and righteous are His judgments, because He has judged the great harlot who corrupted the earth with her fornication; and He has avenged the blood of His servants shed by her'"* (Rev. 19:1-2 NKJV).

Abraham lifted his hand in "hallelujahs" when he had defeated his enemies. The psalmist sang hallelujahs at the thought of the banishment of sin from the earth. The multitude of heaven will worship with hallelujahs at the second coming of Christ and massive defeat of Satan and his Antichrist. Sickness, death, violence, fears, immorality, addictions and every evil thing will be hunted down and banished from the earth for the Millennial restoration. It seems almost unbelievable: One thousand years of hallelujah celebration!

Tribute to God

And how is this "hallelujah" to be proclaimed appropriately? The root word from which the Holy Spirit built this magnificent tribute to God is from the Hebrew *halal* and means to be clear of sound, to shine, to make a show, to boast, and thus to be clamorously foolish; to rave, to celebrate.

For one thousand years this earth is going to ring with clamorously foolish ravings and boasting about Jesus. This revival is a foretaste of that glory, and those who are swimming in the full river of this outpouring are shouting out the high praises of God with a clear sound. Sometimes our people go pouring out of our church for sheer joy and sing in the parking lot so that the neighbors come out of their houses.

Are we acting foolishly? No! We are making a show of His name. Our sound in God's ear is better than the Metropolitan Opera. During our worship services we are clamorously foolish, laughing, dancing, leaping and clapping our hands. One recent evening, in the midst of great celebration, one of our deacons (who was not fully open to the revival at the beginning) stood and, with his hands cupped to his mouth, gave a loud "Tarzan" call! The whole congregation broke out in uproarious laughter.

No sooner had John finished his "Tarzan call" than the Holy Spirit spoke to me saying, *"The world has become a jungle. This is the call to my Church to go out into the darkness and rescue lives that have become entangled with sin and hopelessness."*

Through the liberty and freedom that people are daring to move into during this glorious outpouring, through their shouts of hallelujahs, God is paralyzing the enemy and setting the captives free. Following are just two testimonials of captives who have been gloriously freed during this revival.

Carol's Miracle

In November of 1993 a call came into our church office. "I want to come to one of your services, but I need a ride. I am almost blind." The secretary responded that we would see what we could do, knowing that the caller was an hour away.

We set to work and found a couple in her area who were willing to drive her to the service on Monday evenings. This allowed the woman to continue attending her own church on Sundays. For nine months, this woman periodically came to our services. With the revival in progress, we had more than one opportunity to lay hands on her and pray, although I never met the woman, nor do I remember having seen her. Our Monday evening services are usually sixty percent visitors.

On August 1, 1994, we had been enjoying another wonderful time of worship and teaching and ministry. It was eleven o'clock and the service was coming to a close. About half of the congregation had just left, when I noticed the nearly blind woman with a long metal cane as she was preparing to leave. A voice within me said, "Don't let her leave." Without stopping to think, I ran down the aisle, waving my hand saying, "Wait a minute. Don't let that woman leave yet!" At that same moment a thought came rushing into my mind, "She looks blind! What are you going to do?"

Feeling drained of personal confidence, I began to minister to the woman whatever God put into my heart to say. At my words she threw back her head and began to laugh. I then laid my hand on her upper chest and started to pray. At that same time Pastor Paul walked over and said, "Take off those glasses." He laid his hands on her eyes and said, "In the Name of Jesus, I speak healing to these eyes." We finished praying and walked back down to the altar and continued to minister to others.

Soon we became aware of some kind of conversation going on in the aisle. The blind woman was laughing and going from person to person, saying "I can see your face." Walking up to Pastor Paul, she peered into his eyes and said "I can see Jesus in your eyes!" She turned and walked over to me. "And I can see Jesus in your eyes! I see Jesus in all your eyes!" She then looked down at a small piece of jewelry on my neck and laughed, "I can see that! For one year my sight has been deteriorating. Because of a liver condition, the poisons in my system have affected the optic nerve and I could no longer see with any definition, just mostly outlines of people and things. But tonight, I can see everything clearly defined."

I would like to report here that we all shouted with a great voice of thanksgiving to God. Some did. But Paul and I were stunned. We just stood there looking down at the metal cane lying on our stage.

Erica's Miracle

Three years ago, my nephew Dean Mitchell and his wife Vicki had a beautiful baby girl, their second. When her leg was broken at birth, no one suspected anything but a rapid recovery. The leg refused to heal, however, and the doctors became suspicious. After extensive testing at Birmingham Medical Center, a crushing diagnosis was delivered. Erica had a genetic bone disease.

For three years, Erica has lived in a cast or brace dragging her leg as she faced her life with a sweet, childlike optimism. In March, Dean and Vicki took Erica to the doctor for her regular four-month checkup. This time the sobering prognosis was devastatingly to the point when the doctor said, "After four major operations, the bone graft has still not knit. We can no longer continue to use surgery as a solution to Erica's condition. After her next visit in four months, we will continue to see Erica for her checkups until she is six-years old. At that time we will make a decision. But understand something, amputation of her foot is a possibility."

Many tears and much prayer had gone up for the past three years. Had it all been in vain? Four months went by. One week before Erica was due to return for her checkup, her twelve-year old cousin Brittany was standing in church singing "There's Victory in Jesus" when she began to weep profusely. As soon as the service was over, Brittany rushed home to call Dean and Vicki. "Jesus spoke to me at church tonight," she cried, "I know He is going to heal Erica!"

"That's sweet of you to call," they encouraged her childlike faith.

Erica's aunt and uncle had been taking a walk shortly before Brittany's experience. All of a sudden, the uncle turned to his wife and said, "God is going to heal Erica. I don't know how I know it, but Erica is going to be healed!"

On the Tuesday morning of the miracle, another aunt and uncle who had been praying for Erica in Huntsville, Alabama, were having breakfast. The uncle said to his wife, "Call Dean and Vickie about Erica. They are going to get a good report from the doctor today."

"But they don't go to the doctor this week," his wife responded. "It's next week when they take her."

"Call today!" the uncle insisted. "The Lord brought Erica to me in a dream last night and told me good news is on the way."

In the midst of all these confirmations, Erica fell and injured her crippled leg. Her appointment had to be moved up one week. The doctor would see her on that Tuesday.

So Dean and Vicki drove to Birmingham with Erica. After the doctors completed a thorough examination of the injured leg, the parents were called in for consultation. In total amazement the doctor said, "The X-rays show Erica's bones have knit together! She's not out of the wilderness. It will take some fixing, but she will walk and live a normal life. It's a miracle!"

My brother called in a daze. "God has done a miracle! Erica's leg and ankle bones have knit together!" After much laughing and rejoicing, we said good-bye.

I didn't hear another report until one month later, when I learned that the miracle had an amazing postscript. Because of the disease, the doctor had thought Erica's legs would never be the same in length. One leg was already considerably shorter than the other. "Get set for platform shoes," he had said to them. My brother called with the latest report: "Guess what! Erica's healed leg has grown to within one-eighth inch of the other leg. She not only got a miracle, she's still getting one! Now we have only one more hurdle—that her feet grow to the same length."

Oh, how we laughed and celebrated the mighty God Who has sent His Spirit among us during this beautiful outpouring of His love and power that we have been experiencing!

Two Witnesses From History

In 1821, a lawyer from New York named Charles Finney was dramatically converted. It began when he got interested in the Bible through references to the Mosaic laws in his legal books. He bought a Bible and through reading it, he became intellectually convinced of the truth of Christianity but the question remained—should he become a Christian?

One autumn morning, Finney was on the way to his office when he was stopped in his tracks by an inward voice which seemed to say, *"Will you accept it now, today?"* Instead of going to his office he went off into the woods. Reaching a spot where he thought no one would see him, he knelt down to pray but could not. He was just about to give up when he heard a rustling and looked up in alarm to see if someone had discovered him. And it was then that he realized how great was his pride. Remembering the words of Scripture (Jer. 29:13 KJV), *"Then shall ye seek me, and find me, when ye shall search for me with all your heart,"* he cried out, "Lord, I take Thee at Thy Word."

Finney left the woods in a lighthearted mood. He didn't quite understand what had happened to him. That evening, in the back of his law office, he was overcome with a sense of unutterable ecstasy. He later wrote:

> "The Holy Spirit descended upon me in a manner that seemed to go through me body and soul. I could feel the impression, like a wave of electricity, going through and through me. Indeed, it seemed to come in waves and waves of liquid love, for I could not express it in any other way. It seemed like the very breath of God. I can recollect distinctly that it seemed to fan me, like immense wings."

Finney dropped his law studies the next day and went throughout the town telling what the Lord had done for him. A revival began immediately.

Two women used to sit in Dwight L. Moody's meetings in the front row. He could see by the expressions on their faces that they were praying. At the close of the services, they would say to him: "We have been praying for you."

"Why don't you pray for the people?" Moody would ask.

"Because you need the power of the Spirit," they said.

Years later, Moody said: "I needed the power? Why, I thought I had power. I had the largest congregation in Chicago and there were many conversions. I was in a sense satisfied."

The women kept right on praying, and Moody was filled with a great heart hunger. One evening in New York while trying to raise money for his church which had burned, Moody had an encounter with the Holy Spirit. This was his description of that encounter:

> "My heart was not in the work of begging. I could not appeal. I was crying all the time that God would fill me with His Spirit. Well, one day in the city of New York—oh, what a day!—I cannot describe it. I seldom refer to it; it is almost too sacred an experience to name. Paul had an experience of which he never spoke for fourteen years. I can only say that God revealed himself to me, and I had such an experience of His love that I had to ask Him to stay His hand. I went to preaching again. The sermons were not different; I did not present any new truths, and yet hundreds were converted." (Taken from *America's Great Revivals*, Bethany House, No longer in print.)

What Does it all Mean?

What the full extent of this outpouring of the Holy Spirits means, only God knows. It is refreshing, restorative and encouraging on the one hand; it is invasive, uprooting and purging on the other hand. It is in various Christian denominations across the earth. Yet people of other religions are also encountering Jesus Christ for salvation. Spiritual tremors are rippling simultaneously in many parts.

The systems of man are shaking, both inside the Church and in the world. Every wall is trembling at the sound of a

Giant's footstep. At the liberation of Paris, a soldier recounting that momentous event said: "It was as though a 'Higher Power' had begun to move that no force on earth could stop." Personally, my family and I feel that we have been picked up by something much greater than anything we have ever experienced, and we are moving along with the force of that "Power."

A young woman walked up to me recently and handed me a note. On it was written, *"Man will not stop the revival. I have placed it deep within each man's heart."* This describes precisely what we have experienced since November of 1993. A "Higher Power" has begun to move that no force on earth can stop. God has worked this revival so deeply into our hearts we are being driven along, week by week, into a move that will literally shake the whole earth before it is over.

You have nothing to lose but your pride and your flesh if you would but dare to wade into this outpouring of God's Holy Spirit. You have everything to lose if you refuse. I have never known God to bare himself before the people as He is doing today. Oh that we would strip our own souls and lay open our hearts to His glorious visitation. Surely it is a history shaping opportunity.

Epilogue

Mama is a Methodist!

On Wednesday, February 1, 1995, my mother entered the hospital for the third time in eighteen months. She was facing vascular surgery with a poor prognosis for recovery. At the age of eighty-four, it was a discouraging situation that held no solace except in God. The surgery was long and extensive, beyond what had been anticipated.

On Friday, Mother had survived the surgery and although she was gravely ill, she was lucid and able to be moved into a private room. In the early hours of the morning, one of her sons and his wife who were taking the night watch were awakened by the sound of Mother's voice. One thing that quickly captured their attention was the fact that she was talking out loud, with her eyes wide open, to our father who had died fifteen years earlier. From this point on, Mother relates what was taking place during those early morning hours on February 3, 1995.

"I was lying in my bed, extremely weak and nauseated. I was awake, with my eyes open, when suddenly I slipped out of the bed and into a spacious banqueting room above my head. The room was large and had bleachers like a football field. Yet the bleachers were not crudely built, but were elegant with dainty little backs on each seat. Each row was a gentle tier, one above the other. Each place setting was dressed with beautiful china that had the same pattern as the first set of 'matching dishes' my husband and I bought when our children were young and at home. I was able to confirm that this heavenly china was decorated with the exact same purple flowers because I still have one of the earthly china cups.

"On February 3rd, as I slipped out of my bed and into the room above my head, I met my departed husband and we began to converse while I prepared a meal for him in a small kitchen that was just off the great banqueting area. As I continued to cook, more people began to arrive—children, teenagers and adults. All eight of my children were at this banquet, but I did not recognize the visitors. Yet, as they arrived, each one brought me a gift. The small children brought doll dresses, the youth brought larger dresses and the adults brought even larger garments. As I saw the garments being stacked one upon the other, I became afraid they would become wrinkled. This burdened me to leave the kitchen where I was cooking and attend to the gifts. Yet, as I began to examine the dresses, I saw they were made of an exquisite, wrinkle-free material. They were delicate and beautiful, perfectly made, even in the doll dresses, every stitch was sewn with a perfection far beyond man's finest work.

"Then I left the dining area and went back into my bed in the hospital room. Once in my bed, I looked over at the window and standing in front of it were two of the most beautiful beings I have ever seen. They had the appearance of a bride and one was larger than the other. I suppose they were angels. Their robes, or garments, were pure white like snow and made of solid lace. It was a delicate lace that was intricately woven. Their hair was dark black, about shoulder length, and they had large, dark brown eyes. A mist was around the two angels.

"Whenever they moved, their arms were locked in a friendship embrace, and everywhere I looked in the room, they were there. Sometimes the angels were in front of my son and his wife, sometimes they were behind them. Whenever I would go back into the dining room at the top of my bed, I would not see the angels. But when I returned to my bed, they were there.

"From time to time, the angels would pass back and forth across the room. As they moved, they did not walk as we do, but they seemed to glide. Sometimes they would pass all the way through the door and into the hallway and then they would return. From time to time, the angels would look at me. They would look directly into my eyes and I would look directly into theirs. Their expression was kind and gentle.

"By 5:00 a.m., I had passed from the banqueting room for the last time. From my bed, I watched the two angels glide by my feet, out the door and then disappear into the hospital corridor. I was fully awake and began talking with my son and his wife."

My brother immediately spoke to my mother, saying, "Mother, you have been talking to Daddy."

"I know."

"You were cooking for him."

"I know that, too." With those words, Mother began to relate her unusual experience to them. "Tonight I have had visitors in this room. Sometimes they were in front of you and sometimes they passed behind you. I was awake through it all. I could see you responding to my talking with your Daddy, but I didn't realize at the time what was really happening. It all seemed so natural, but in fact, I have had a visitation of angels."

There is a thin veil that hangs between this natural world and the spirit world that surrounds us. The New Testament declares that angels are "... *ministering spirits, sent forth to minister for them who shall be heirs of salvation*" (Heb. 1:14 KJV). What happened to my mother has happened to others since recorded time. The Bible gives record of numerous visitations of angels to this planet.

On the night of my mother's visitation, she was obviously passing back and forth between this world and the spirit realm. Each time she entered the great banqueting room, her spirit was slipping out of her body. But God was not ready for her to leave this earth, and He sent angels to minister strength into her physical body. I am sure that each time the angels looked into my mother's eyes, divine strength was being imparted. Once her condition had fully stabilized, the angels departed for another mission or returned back to glory.

After giving considerable thought to each scene of this heavenly visitation, I believe that my mother's visit to the heavenly banqueting room was a glimpse of the joyous celebration and rewards that await her long faithful life. She never wrote a book, nor filled a formal pulpit, but opportunity became the pulpit from which my mother has reached out to people of every age and strata of life, as far back as I can remember. Together, she and my father trained up our extended family of fifty-six offspring in the ways of God. They lifted up the community in which they lived. They strengthened the Methodist church where they were lifelong members. And they always reverenced the name of Jesus above any financial blessing they may have been able to enjoy in life. The visitors mother saw at the banqueting table were surely the countless souls she and my father touched through their fifty years together on this earth.

The one seemingly different feature of this whole encounter that has impressed my heart most is the china. I have cried a flood of tears every time I have thought of the sheer possibility of what that means. When my parents married, they had $14.00 with which to buy furniture and household goods. Riding in a Model T, they set out to start their life together in the red clay hills of Alabama. Working in a rural setting that was backbreaking at times, they fought poverty of body and soul until they were able to bring their family into a wonderful standard of living.

Rooted in church, trained on biblical principles of humility and hard work, a set of "matching dishes" was one of my parents' most prized possessions. The peace and the dignity of a fine table was pivotal to our family. It allowed us to serve those who passed through our home with a sense of accomplishment and satisfaction. And although I didn't realize it at the time, the Bible places considerable emphasis on dining together. Jesus himself declared He will sit with us in His coming kingdom (see Luke 22:16).

To think that the God of all creation would bother to see that the pattern of my mother's precious first set of china would be the pattern on the china of her heavenly awards banquet is mind boggling. Heaven and earth are much closer than we think. Many scholars agree that the book of Genesis suggests the vegetation on earth was transplanted from Paradise.

I believe the Church is coming into a time when it will experience more manifestations of the Holy Spirit, more signs and wonders, more angelic visitations, more dreams and visions, than it ever has before. I am fully aware that such a statement causes many to quake for fear of excess.

But how can we presume to quench the very things the Lord said would precede His return?

The Church is focused upon the Church. This is the problem. We are trying to assess revival based on man. Today, as I am penning the last page of this book, the Holy Spirit spoke a statement into my understanding that should clear up any remaining confusion:

"Genuine revival is a revival of the works of God."

God revives **His own works**—in the midst of the people. We then see those works being manifested through the people. It is the works and stirrings of God that we are witnessing at this time of revival. God never looks into the Church or the world and says to His Holy Spirit, *"Go stir up those people."* He looks instead upon the human scene and says to the Holy Spirit, "Go stir up my works among the people!" Then all who are hungry sense the stirring and began to swim in the life-giving waters.

Mona Johnian, along with her husband, Senior Pastor Paul Johnian, M.M., is co-founder of the Christian Teaching and Worship Center and Kaleo Bible Institute. Mona has been a pulpit minister and conference speaker for the past 18 years. She teaches Eschatology, Old Testament Survey and Theology at Kaleo Bible Institute. Paul and Mona are seen and heard on radio and television in the Boston area. Their church on the North Shore of Boston has been in revival since 1993 with spiritual signs and wonders.

To order books and tapes by Mona Johnian or to contact her for speaking engagements, please call or write:

MONA JOHNIAN
Christian Teaching and Worship Center
73 Pine Street
Woburn, MA 01801
(617) 935-5117

Other Books by Mona Johnian

The Fresh Anointing—\$6.95
A bestseller! Endorsed by Richard Roberts. Investigating the outpouring of the Holy Spirit today.

Life in the Millennium—\$7.95
Endorsed by Jack Van Impe as one of the most comprehensive books available on the subject of the coming millennium.

Renewing Your Mind—\$6.95
A bestseller! Endorsed by Len LeSourd. A commonsense approach to sound thinking.

Winning the Battle in Your Mind—\$3.50
Spiritual warfare in the battleground of the mind.

SOON TO BE RELEASED! (Bridge Publishing)
Signs and Wonders—Taking Scriptures that have been buried under years of tradition and present-day experiences to explain the phenomena of signs and wonders in the Church today. Read, be informed and thrilled!

"Impact for Living" Booklets

Heaven—\$7.00
a series of 7 booklets on Heaven

The Voice of God—\$7.00
A series of 7 booklets on hearing from God.

The Coming Waves of Power—\$1.00
Christ vs. Antichrist

The Coming Antichrist—\$1.25
A profile of the coming political genius.

The Parable of the Ten Virgins—\$1.00
Outstanding insight into this mysterious parable.

For a complete list of books, please write for a free catalogue:

MONA JOHNIAN

Christian Teaching and Worship Center

73 Pine Street Woburn, MA 01801

Kaleo Bible Institute

Historic Boston—Home of the First Great Awakening

Kaleo is a one year international Bible school that equips and trains people who are called into full-time ministry as well as lay people. Kaleo offers two programs— Ministerial Studies and Bible Enrichment as well as part-time studies and auditing. All courses are taught by professors and ministers with excellent academic and spiritual qualifications.

- First Quarter—Bibliology. The study of the Bible, Scriptures, Old and New Testament Survey and all related courses.
- Second Quarter—Theology. The study of Christ and God, the impact of Christ on our life and all related courses.
- Third and Fourth Quarters—Pneumotology, the study of the Holy Spirit. Signs and wonders, gifts of the Spirit, motivational gifts, fruit of the Spirit, worship, revivals past, **present-day revival** and all related courses.

- Special revival opportunities. A chance to bring revival to surrounding states and other countries.
- Financial assistance to qualifying students
- Registration deadline — September 5, 1995
- Kaleo Bible Institute is a member of ORUEF
  (Oral Roberts University Educational Fellowship)

For more information or a catalog, please call or write:
Kaleo Bible Institute
73 Pine Street, Woburn, MA 01801, (617) 935-5117